**TEACHER'S PET PUBLICATIONS**

PUZZLE PACK
for
Black Boy
based on the book by
Richard Wright

Written by
William T. Collins

© 2005 Teacher's Pet Publications
All Rights Reserved

The materials in this packet are copyrighted
by Teacher's Pet Publications, Inc.

These pages may be duplicated by the purchaser
for use in the purchaser's own classroom.

Copying any of these materials and distributing them
for any other purpose is a violation of the copyright laws.

© 2005 Teacher's Pet Publications, Inc.
www.tpet.com

INTRODUCTION

If you already own the LitPlan for this title, this Puzzle Pack will refresh your Unit Resource Materials and Vocabulary Resource Materials sections plus give you additional materials you can substitute into the tests. If you do not already have a complete LitPlan, these pages will give you some supplemental materials to use with your own plan. There are two main groups of materials: one set for unit words (such as characters' names, symbols, places, etc.) and one set for vocabulary words associated with the book.

WORD LIST

There is a word list for both the unit words and the vocabulary words. These lists show you which words are being used in the materials and the clues or definitions being used for those words. You may want to give students a word list with clues/definitions to help them, or you may want students to only have a word list (without clues/definitions) if you want them to work a little harder. Both are available for duplication. The word lists can also be your "calling key" for the bingo games.

FILL IN THE BLANK AND MATCHING

There are 4 each of the fill in the blank and matching worksheets for both the unit and vocabulary words. These pages can be used either as extra worksheets for students or as objective parts of a unit test. They can be done individually if students need extra help or as a whole class activity to review the material covered.

MAGIC SQUARES

The magic squares not only reinforce the material covered but also work on reasoning and math skills. Many teachers have told us that their students really enjoy doing these!

WORD SEARCH PUZZLES

The word search words go in all directions, as indicated on your answer keys. Two of the word search puzzles have the clues listed rather than the words. This makes the puzzle a little more difficult, but it reinforces the material better. Two word search puzzles have words only for students who find the clue puzzles too difficult.

CROSSWORD PUZZLES

Both unit and vocabulary word sections have 4 crossword puzzles.

BINGO CARDS

There are 32 individual bingo cards for the unit words and 32 individual bingo cards for the vocabulary words. You can use your word list as a "call list," calling the words at random and marking them off of your list as you go, or you could use the flash cards by cutting them apart and drawing the words at random from a hat (or box or whatever). To make a better review, you might ask for the definition and spelling of each word as you call it out–or you could call out the definitions and have students tell you the words they need to look for on the puzzle.

JUGGLE LETTERS

The vocabulary juggle letter game is intended to help students learn the spellings of the words. One sheet has the definitions listed on it as an extra help for students who need it or to reinforce the definitions if you choose to do so.

FLASH CARDS

We've included a set of vocabulary flash cards you can duplicate, cut, and fold for your students. Some teachers make a few sets for general use by the class; others make a set for each student. Some teachers duplicate them for each student and have the students cut & fold their own. You can cut out just the words and put them in a hat, have each student pick out one word and write the definition and a sentence for that word. Students then swap words and papers, with the next student adding a sentence of his own under the last one. You can have students swap as many times as you like. Each time the student will read the sentences written prior to his own and then add a sentence. You can cut out the words and definitions separately and play "I Have; Who Has?" Each student in the room draws a word and definition. The first student says, "I have (the name of the word). Who has the definition?" The student with the definition reads it then says, "I have (the name of the vocabulary word she has). Who has the definition?" The round continues until all words and definitions have been given.

Black Boy Unit Word List

No.	Word	Clue/Definition
1.	ADDIE	Granny's ally; Richard's teacher
2.	ALLY	Aunt Addie was Granny's ____
3.	ANGEL	If Richard had seen an ____ like Jacob had, he would have believed, too
4.	AUNT	Addie or Maggie to Richard
5.	BAPTIZED	Richard agreed to be ____ into the church to please his mother
6.	BESS	Willing to marry Richard
7.	CLARK	Takes Richard to live in Greenwood
8.	COUNT	The coal man taught Richard to ____
9.	CRANE	Good-hearted white employer at optical company
10.	CURTAINS	Little Richard set these on fire
11.	DEATH	'The penalty of ____ awaited me if I make a false move...'
12.	DIED	A boy had ____ in Richard's bed at Uncle Clark's house
13.	ELEVATOR	Shorty operated one
14.	ELLA	Richard's mother
15.	FALK	Helped Richard get library books
16.	GRANDPA	A Civil War veteran
17.	GRANNY	Strict Seventh-Day Adventist with whom Richard often lives
18.	GREENWOOD	Uncle Clark & Aunt Jody lived there
19.	GRIGGS	Richard's classmate who gives him advice
20.	HARRISON	Agrees to fight Richard for money
21.	HELENA	Wrights had to move from West ____
22.	INSURANCE	Brother Manse's work
23.	JUDGE	Ruled in Richard's father's favor in court
24.	KITTEN	Richard hanged it to get back at his father
25.	KNIFE	Richard defended himself against Aunt Addie with one
26.	MAGGIE	Richard's favorite aunt
27.	MARRY	Mrs. Moss wanted Bess to ____ Richard
28.	MEMPHIS	Home town of Mrs. Moss and Bess
29.	MENCKEN	Author/editor who intrigued Richard
30.	MONEY	Richard took part in a scheme that skimmed ____ from ticket sales
31.	MOSS	Landlady in Memphis
32.	NATHANIEL	Richard's father
33.	NEWSPAPERS	Richard sold 'anti-Negro' ____
34.	NORTH	'It symbolized to me all I had not felt and seen....'
35.	OLIN	Set up fight between Richard and Harrison
36.	ORPHAN	Richard had to go to an ____'s home when his mother became ill
37.	PRETEND	Richard and Harrison agreed to ____ to fight
38.	RAZORS	Richard threatened to cut Uncle Tom with ____
39.	REYNOLDS	Threatened Richard & forced him to leave his good job
40.	RICHARD	Black boy is about him
41.	SALOON	Place where Richard passed time at age 6
42.	SELL	Richard tried to ____ Bessie
43.	SHORTY	Elevator operator
44.	SHOT	White men ____ Uncle Hoskins
45.	SIMON	Head of the orphanage
46.	SINFUL	Granny thought story books were ____
47.	SOLDIERS	Richard saw these & prisoners when returning to Granny's
48.	SPEECH	Richard refused to deliver the prewritten graduation ____
49.	SYMBOL	'My mother's suffering grew into a ____ in my mind....'
50.	THINK	Advice Griggs gave Richard

Black Boy Unit Word List

No.	Word	Clue/Definition
51.	THOMAS	Richard threatened him with razors
52.	TOWEL	Granny hit Richard with one when he told her to 'kiss back there'
53.	VOODOO	'The ____ of Hell's Half-Acre'
54.	WRIGHT	Author's last name

Black Boy Fill In The Blank 1

_____

_____

_____

_____

_____

_____

_____

_____

_____

_____

_____

_____

_____

_____

_____

_____

_____

_____

_____

_____

1. Granny's ally; Richard's teacher
2. Little Richard set these on fire
3. Granny hit Richard with one when he told her to 'kiss back there'
4. Richard saw these & prisoners when returning to Granny's
5. Richard took part in a scheme that skimmed ____ from ticket sales
6. Wrights had to move from West ____
7. Strict Seventh-Day Adventist with whom Richard often lives
8. Shorty operated one
9. Helped Richard get library books
10. Richard tried to ____ Bessie
11. Richard's mother
12. Willing to marry Richard
13. Takes Richard to live in Greenwood
14. 'My mother's suffering grew into a ____ in my mind....'
15. If Richard had seen an ____ like Jacob had, he would have believed, too
16. Place where Richard passed time at age 6
17. Author's last name
18. A Civil War veteran
19. Addie or Maggie to Richard
20. The coal man taught Richard to ____

Black Boy Fill In The Blank 1 Answer Key

ADDIE	1. Granny's ally; Richard's teacher
CURTAINS	2. Little Richard set these on fire
TOWEL	3. Granny hit Richard with one when he told her to 'kiss back there'
SOLDIERS	4. Richard saw these & prisoners when returning to Granny's
MONEY	5. Richard took part in a scheme that skimmed ____ from ticket sales
HELENA	6. Wrights had to move from West ____
GRANNY	7. Strict Seventh-Day Adventist with whom Richard often lives
ELEVATOR	8. Shorty operated one
FALK	9. Helped Richard get library books
SELL	10. Richard tried to ____ Bessie
ELLA	11. Richard's mother
BESS	12. Willing to marry Richard
CLARK	13. Takes Richard to live in Greenwood
SYMBOL	14. 'My mother's suffering grew into a ____ in my mind....'
ANGEL	15. If Richard had seen an ____ like Jacob had, he would have believed, too
SALOON	16. Place where Richard passed time at age 6
WRIGHT	17. Author's last name
GRANDPA	18. A Civil War veteran
AUNT	19. Addie or Maggie to Richard
COUNT	20. The coal man taught Richard to ____

Black Boy Fill In The Blank 2

_____

1. Addie or Maggie to Richard
2. Granny thought story books were ____
3. Black boy is about him
4. Strict Seventh-Day Adventist with whom Richard often lives
5. Helped Richard get library books
6. The coal man taught Richard to ____
7. Richard refused to deliver the prewritten graduation ____
8. Shorty operated one
9. Richard's classmate who gives him advice
10. Mrs. Moss wanted Bess to ____ Richard
11. Richard's mother
12. 'The penalty of ____ awaited me if I make a false move...'
13. Richard saw these & prisoners when returning to Granny's
14. Home town of Mrs. Moss and Bess
15. A boy had ____ in Richard's bed at Uncle Clark's house
16. Threatened Richard & forced him to leave his good job
17. Wrights had to move from West ____
18. Richard threatened him with razors
19. Ruled in Richard's father's favor in court
20. Richard's father

Black Boy Fill In The Blank 2 Answer Key

AUNT	1. Addie or Maggie to Richard
SINFUL	2. Granny thought story books were ____
RICHARD	3. Black boy is about him
GRANNY	4. Strict Seventh-Day Adventist with whom Richard often lives
FALK	5. Helped Richard get library books
COUNT	6. The coal man taught Richard to ____
SPEECH	7. Richard refused to deliver the prewritten graduation ____
ELEVATOR	8. Shorty operated one
GRIGGS	9. Richard's classmate who gives him advice
MARRY	10. Mrs. Moss wanted Bess to ____ Richard
ELLA	11. Richard's mother
DEATH	12. 'The penalty of ____ awaited me if I make a false move...'
SOLDIERS	13. Richard saw these & prisoners when returning to Granny's
MEMPHIS	14. Home town of Mrs. Moss and Bess
DIED	15. A boy had ____ in Richard's bed at Uncle Clark's house
REYNOLDS	16. Threatened Richard & forced him to leave his good job
HELENA	17. Wrights had to move from West ____
THOMAS	18. Richard threatened him with razors
JUDGE	19. Ruled in Richard's father's favor in court
NATHANIEL	20. Richard's father

Black Boy Fill In The Blank 3

_____

_____

_____

_____

_____

_____

_____

_____

_____

_____

_____

_____

_____

_____

_____

_____

_____

_____

_____

_____

1. Advice Griggs gave Richard
2. 'The penalty of ____ awaited me if I make a false move...'
3. Granny's ally; Richard's teacher
4. A Civil War veteran
5. Aunt Addie was Granny's____
6. Wrights had to move from West ____
7. Richard agreed to be ____ into the church to please his mother
8. Willing to marry Richard
9. Landlady in Memphis
10. Richard refused to deliver the prewritten graduation ____
11. Author/editor who intrigued Richard
12. Good-hearted white employer at optical company
13. The coal man taught Richard to ____
14. A boy had ____ in Richard's bed at Uncle Clark's house
15. Little Richard set these on fire
16. If Richard had seen an ____ like Jacob had, he would have believed, too
17. Richard tried to ____ Bessie
18. Richard's father
19. Agrees to fight Richard for money
20. Granny hit Richard with one when he told her to 'kiss back there'

Black Boy Fill In The Blank 3 Answer Key

THINK	1. Advice Griggs gave Richard
DEATH	2. 'The penalty of ____ awaited me if I make a false move...'
ADDIE	3. Granny's ally; Richard's teacher
GRANDPA	4. A Civil War veteran
ALLY	5. Aunt Addie was Granny's____
HELENA	6. Wrights had to move from West ____
BAPTIZED	7. Richard agreed to be ____ into the church to please his mother
BESS	8. Willing to marry Richard
MOSS	9. Landlady in Memphis
SPEECH	10. Richard refused to deliver the prewritten graduation ____
MENCKEN	11. Author/editor who intrigued Richard
CRANE	12. Good-hearted white employer at optical company
COUNT	13. The coal man taught Richard to ____
DIED	14. A boy had ____ in Richard's bed at Uncle Clark's house
CURTAINS	15. Little Richard set these on fire
ANGEL	16. If Richard had seen an ____ like Jacob had, he would have believed, too
SELL	17. Richard tried to ____ Bessie
NATHANIEL	18. Richard's father
HARRISON	19. Agrees to fight Richard for money
TOWEL	20. Granny hit Richard with one when he told her to 'kiss back there'

Black Boy Fill In The Blank 4

_____

_____

_____

_____

_____

_____

_____

_____

_____

_____

_____

_____

_____

_____

_____

_____

_____

_____

_____

_____

1. Little Richard set these on fire
2. Richard took part in a scheme that skimmed ____ from ticket sales
3. Richard hanged it to get back at his father
4. Advice Griggs gave Richard
5. Set up fight between Richard and Harrison
6. Granny's ally; Richard's teacher
7. 'My mother's suffering grew into a ____ in my mind....'
8. Granny hit Richard with one when he told her to 'kiss back there'
9. A Civil War veteran
10. Takes Richard to live in Greenwood
11. Landlady in Memphis
12. Willing to marry Richard
13. Elevator operator
14. Richard sold 'anti-Negro' ____
15. 'The ____ of Hell's Half-Acre'
16. Richard and Harrison agreed to ____ to fight
17. Richard tried to ____ Bessie
18. Richard threatened to cut Uncle Tom with ____
19. Richard's favorite aunt
20. Threatened Richard & forced him to leave his good job

Black Boy Fill In The Blank 4 Answer Key

CURTAINS	1. Little Richard set these on fire
MONEY	2. Richard took part in a scheme that skimmed ____ from ticket sales
KITTEN	3. Richard hanged it to get back at his father
THINK	4. Advice Griggs gave Richard
OLIN	5. Set up fight between Richard and Harrison
ADDIE	6. Granny's ally; Richard's teacher
SYMBOL	7. 'My mother's suffering grew into a ____ in my mind....'
TOWEL	8. Granny hit Richard with one when he told her to 'kiss back there'
GRANDPA	9. A Civil War veteran
CLARK	10. Takes Richard to live in Greenwood
MOSS	11. Landlady in Memphis
BESS	12. Willing to marry Richard
SHORTY	13. Elevator operator
NEWSPAPERS	14. Richard sold 'anti-Negro' ____
VOODOO	15. 'The ____ of Hell's Half-Acre'
PRETEND	16. Richard and Harrison agreed to ____ to fight
SELL	17. Richard tried to ____ Bessie
RAZORS	18. Richard threatened to cut Uncle Tom with ____
MAGGIE	19. Richard's favorite aunt
REYNOLDS	20. Threatened Richard & forced him to leave his good job

Black Boy Matching 1

___ 1. CLARK   A. Richard sold 'anti-Negro' ____
___ 2. REYNOLDS   B. Richard took part in a scheme that skimmed ____ from ticket sales
___ 3. HELENA   C. Agrees to fight Richard for money
___ 4. TOWEL   D. Uncle Clark & Aunt Jody lived there
___ 5. NEWSPAPERS   E. Shorty operated one
___ 6. SINFUL   F. Author's last name
___ 7. KITTEN   G. Author/editor who intrigued Richard
___ 8. NATHANIEL   H. Richard threatened to cut Uncle Tom with ____
___ 9. HARRISON   I. Richard defended himself against Aunt Addie with one
___10. CURTAINS   J. Home town of Mrs. Moss and Bess
___11. MOSS   K. Richard's father
___12. CRANE   L. Landlady in Memphis
___13. MEMPHIS   M. Wrights had to move from West ____
___14. MONEY   N. Little Richard set these on fire
___15. SOLDIERS   O. Granny hit Richard with one when he told her to 'kiss back there'
___16. OLIN   P. Takes Richard to live in Greenwood
___17. GRANDPA   Q. Willing to marry Richard
___18. KNIFE   R. Richard saw these & prisoners when returning to Granny's
___19. MENCKEN   S. Good-hearted white employer at optical company
___20. ELEVATOR   T. Granny thought story books were ____
___21. RAZORS   U. Set up fight between Richard and Harrison
___22. BESS   V. A Civil War veteran
___23. WRIGHT   W. Ruled in Richard's father's favor in court
___24. GREENWOOD   X. Threatened Richard & forced him to leave his good job
___25. JUDGE   Y. Richard hanged it to get back at his father

Black Boy Matching 1 Answer Key

P - 1. CLARK	A.	Richard sold 'anti-Negro' ____
X - 2. REYNOLDS	B.	Richard took part in a scheme that skimmed ____ from ticket sales
M - 3. HELENA	C.	Agrees to fight Richard for money
O - 4. TOWEL	D.	Uncle Clark & Aunt Jody lived there
A - 5. NEWSPAPERS	E.	Shorty operated one
T - 6. SINFUL	F.	Author's last name
Y - 7. KITTEN	G.	Author/editor who intrigued Richard
K - 8. NATHANIEL	H.	Richard threatened to cut Uncle Tom with ____
C - 9. HARRISON	I.	Richard defended himself against Aunt Addie with one
N -10. CURTAINS	J.	Home town of Mrs. Moss and Bess
L -11. MOSS	K.	Richard's father
S -12. CRANE	L.	Landlady in Memphis
J -13. MEMPHIS	M.	Wrights had to move from West ____
B -14. MONEY	N.	Little Richard set these on fire
R -15. SOLDIERS	O.	Granny hit Richard with one when he told her to 'kiss back there'
U -16. OLIN	P.	Takes Richard to live in Greenwood
V -17. GRANDPA	Q.	Willing to marry Richard
I -18. KNIFE	R.	Richard saw these & prisoners when returning to Granny's
G -19. MENCKEN	S.	Good-hearted white employer at optical company
E -20. ELEVATOR	T.	Granny thought story books were ____
H -21. RAZORS	U.	Set up fight between Richard and Harrison
Q -22. BESS	V.	A Civil War veteran
F -23. WRIGHT	W.	Ruled in Richard's father's favor in court
D -24. GREENWOOD	X.	Threatened Richard & forced him to leave his good job
W -25. JUDGE	Y.	Richard hanged it to get back at his father

Black Boy Matching 2

___ 1. REYNOLDS   A. Agrees to fight Richard for money
___ 2. SELL   B. Wrights had to move from West ____
___ 3. MENCKEN   C. Advice Griggs gave Richard
___ 4. GREENWOOD   D. Richard tried to ____ Bessie
___ 5. CURTAINS   E. Aunt Addie was Granny's____
___ 6. CLARK   F. Threatened Richard & forced him to leave his good job
___ 7. SOLDIERS   G. Black boy is about him
___ 8. DEATH   H. Elevator operator
___ 9. SINFUL   I. Author/editor who intrigued Richard
___ 10. MOSS   J. Richard threatened to cut Uncle Tom with ____
___ 11. MAGGIE   K. 'The penalty of ____ awaited me if I make a false move...'
___ 12. WRIGHT   L. Richard defended himself against Aunt Addie with one
___ 13. RICHARD   M. Strict Seventh-Day Adventist with whom Richard often lives
___ 14. HARRISON   N. Granny thought story books were ____
___ 15. ALLY   O. 'It symbolized to me all I had not felt and seen....'
___ 16. SHORTY   P. Landlady in Memphis
___ 17. GRANNY   Q. Richard had to go to an ____'s home when his mother became ill
___ 18. FALK   R. Richard saw these & prisoners when returning to Granny's
___ 19. COUNT   S. Little Richard set these on fire
___ 20. NORTH   T. Uncle Clark & Aunt Jody lived there
___ 21. RAZORS   U. Helped Richard get library books
___ 22. HELENA   V. Takes Richard to live in Greenwood
___ 23. ORPHAN   W. The coal man taught Richard to ____
___ 24. THINK   X. Author's last name
___ 25. KNIFE   Y. Richard's favorite aunt

Black Boy Matching 2 Answer Key

F - 1.	REYNOLDS	A. Agrees to fight Richard for money
D - 2.	SELL	B. Wrights had to move from West ____
I - 3.	MENCKEN	C. Advice Griggs gave Richard
T - 4.	GREENWOOD	D. Richard tried to ____ Bessie
S - 5.	CURTAINS	E. Aunt Addie was Granny's ____
V - 6.	CLARK	F. Threatened Richard & forced him to leave his good job
R - 7.	SOLDIERS	G. Black boy is about him
K - 8.	DEATH	H. Elevator operator
N - 9.	SINFUL	I. Author/editor who intrigued Richard
P - 10.	MOSS	J. Richard threatened to cut Uncle Tom with ____
Y - 11.	MAGGIE	K. 'The penalty of ____ awaited me if I make a false move...'
X - 12.	WRIGHT	L. Richard defended himself against Aunt Addie with one
G - 13.	RICHARD	M. Strict Seventh-Day Adventist with whom Richard often lives
A - 14.	HARRISON	N. Granny thought story books were ____
E - 15.	ALLY	O. 'It symbolized to me all I had not felt and seen....'
H - 16.	SHORTY	P. Landlady in Memphis
M - 17.	GRANNY	Q. Richard had to go to an ____'s home when his mother became ill
U - 18.	FALK	R. Richard saw these & prisoners when returning to Granny's
W - 19.	COUNT	S. Little Richard set these on fire
O - 20.	NORTH	T. Uncle Clark & Aunt Jody lived there
J - 21.	RAZORS	U. Helped Richard get library books
B - 22.	HELENA	V. Takes Richard to live in Greenwood
Q - 23.	ORPHAN	W. The coal man taught Richard to ____
C - 24.	THINK	X. Author's last name
L - 25.	KNIFE	Y. Richard's favorite aunt

Black Boy Matching 3

___ 1. SYMBOL   A. Richard saw these & prisoners when returning to Granny's
___ 2. NEWSPAPERS   B. Richard took part in a scheme that skimmed ____ from ticket sales
___ 3. GRANNY   C. Richard agreed to be ____ into the church to please his mother
___ 4. SIMON   D. 'It symbolized to me all I had not felt and seen....'
___ 5. GRIGGS   E. Shorty operated one
___ 6. SHOT   F. Head of the orphanage
___ 7. BAPTIZED   G. Richard tried to ____ Bessie
___ 8. CURTAINS   H. White men ____ Uncle Hoskins
___ 9. GREENWOOD   I. Author/editor who intrigued Richard
___10. MEMPHIS   J. 'My mother's suffering grew into a ____ in my mind....'
___11. WRIGHT   K. Richard defended himself against Aunt Addie with one
___12. SOLDIERS   L. Aunt Addie was Granny's ____
___13. THOMAS   M. Helped Richard get library books
___14. ELEVATOR   N. Uncle Clark & Aunt Jody lived there
___15. ORPHAN   O. Place where Richard passed time at age 6
___16. MENCKEN   P. Richard's classmate who gives him advice
___17. AUNT   Q. Richard had to go to an ____'s home when his mother became ill
___18. REYNOLDS   R. Addie or Maggie to Richard
___19. SALOON   S. Threatened Richard & forced him to leave his good job
___20. MONEY   T. Richard threatened him with razors
___21. ALLY   U. Strict Seventh-Day Adventist with whom Richard often lives
___22. KNIFE   V. Richard sold 'anti-Negro' ____
___23. SELL   W. Home town of Mrs. Moss and Bess
___24. NORTH   X. Author's last name
___25. FALK   Y. Little Richard set these on fire

Black Boy Matching 3 Answer Key

J - 1. SYMBOL	A.	Richard saw these & prisoners when returning to Granny's
V - 2. NEWSPAPERS	B.	Richard took part in a scheme that skimmed ____ from ticket sales
U - 3. GRANNY	C.	Richard agreed to be ____ into the church to please his mother
F - 4. SIMON	D.	'It symbolized to me all I had not felt and seen....'
P - 5. GRIGGS	E.	Shorty operated one
H - 6. SHOT	F.	Head of the orphanage
C - 7. BAPTIZED	G.	Richard tried to ____ Bessie
Y - 8. CURTAINS	H.	White men ____ Uncle Hoskins
N - 9. GREENWOOD	I.	Author/editor who intrigued Richard
W - 10. MEMPHIS	J.	'My mother's suffering grew into a ____ in my mind....'
X - 11. WRIGHT	K.	Richard defended himself against Aunt Addie with one
A - 12. SOLDIERS	L.	Aunt Addie was Granny's ____
T - 13. THOMAS	M.	Helped Richard get library books
E - 14. ELEVATOR	N.	Uncle Clark & Aunt Jody lived there
Q - 15. ORPHAN	O.	Place where Richard passed time at age 6
I - 16. MENCKEN	P.	Richard's classmate who gives him advice
R - 17. AUNT	Q.	Richard had to go to an ____'s home when his mother became ill
S - 18. REYNOLDS	R.	Addie or Maggie to Richard
O - 19. SALOON	S.	Threatened Richard & forced him to leave his good job
B - 20. MONEY	T.	Richard threatened him with razors
L - 21. ALLY	U.	Strict Seventh-Day Adventist with whom Richard often lives
K - 22. KNIFE	V.	Richard sold 'anti-Negro' ____
G - 23. SELL	W.	Home town of Mrs. Moss and Bess
D - 24. NORTH	X.	Author's last name
M - 25. FALK	Y.	Little Richard set these on fire

Black Boy Matching 4

___ 1. ELLA   A. Richard threatened to cut Uncle Tom with ____
___ 2. COUNT   B. A Civil War veteran
___ 3. MEMPHIS   C. A boy had ____ in Richard's bed at Uncle Clark's house
___ 4. THOMAS   D. 'The ____ of Hell's Half-Acre'
___ 5. SIMON   E. Little Richard set these on fire
___ 6. SELL   F. Black boy is about him
___ 7. NORTH   G. Richard's mother
___ 8. GRANNY   H. Richard took part in a scheme that skimmed ____ from ticket sales
___ 9. PRETEND   I. Ruled in Richard's father's favor in court
___10. BAPTIZED   J. Richard's classmate who gives him advice
___11. JUDGE   K. 'My mother's suffering grew into a ____ in my mind....'
___12. VOODOO   L. Uncle Clark & Aunt Jody lived there
___13. RICHARD   M. Granny's ally; Richard's teacher
___14. ADDIE   N. Richard and Harrison agreed to ____ to fight
___15. GREENWOOD   O. Granny thought story books were ____
___16. GRIGGS   P. Richard agreed to be ____ into the church to please his mother
___17. SALOON   Q. The coal man taught Richard to ____
___18. CURTAINS   R. Strict Seventh-Day Adventist with whom Richard often lives
___19. SINFUL   S. Richard threatened him with razors
___20. SHORTY   T. Richard tried to ____ Bessie
___21. MONEY   U. Place where Richard passed time at age 6
___22. DIED   V. Home town of Mrs. Moss and Bess
___23. GRANDPA   W. Head of the orphanage
___24. RAZORS   X. 'It symbolized to me all I had not felt and seen....'
___25. SYMBOL   Y. Elevator operator

Black Boy Matching 4 Answer Key

G - 1.	ELLA	A. Richard threatened to cut Uncle Tom with ____
Q - 2.	COUNT	B. A Civil War veteran
V - 3.	MEMPHIS	C. A boy had ____ in Richard's bed at Uncle Clark's house
S - 4.	THOMAS	D. 'The ____ of Hell's Half-Acre'
W - 5.	SIMON	E. Little Richard set these on fire
T - 6.	SELL	F. Black boy is about him
X - 7.	NORTH	G. Richard's mother
R - 8.	GRANNY	H. Richard took part in a scheme that skimmed ____ from ticket sales
N - 9.	PRETEND	I. Ruled in Richard's father's favor in court
P - 10.	BAPTIZED	J. Richard's classmate who gives him advice
I - 11.	JUDGE	K. 'My mother's suffering grew into a ____ in my mind....'
D - 12.	VOODOO	L. Uncle Clark & Aunt Jody lived there
F - 13.	RICHARD	M. Granny's ally; Richard's teacher
M - 14.	ADDIE	N. Richard and Harrison agreed to ____ to fight
L - 15.	GREENWOOD	O. Granny thought story books were ____
J - 16.	GRIGGS	P. Richard agreed to be ____ into the church to please his mother
U - 17.	SALOON	Q. The coal man taught Richard to ____
E - 18.	CURTAINS	R. Strict Seventh-Day Adventist with whom Richard often lives
O - 19.	SINFUL	S. Richard threatened him with razors
Y - 20.	SHORTY	T. Richard tried to ____ Bessie
H - 21.	MONEY	U. Place where Richard passed time at age 6
C - 22.	DIED	V. Home town of Mrs. Moss and Bess
B - 23.	GRANDPA	W. Head of the orphanage
A - 24.	RAZORS	X. 'It symbolized to me all I had not felt and seen....'
K - 25.	SYMBOL	Y. Elevator operator

Copyrighted

Black Boy Magic Squares 1

Match the definition with the vocabulary word. Put your answers in the magic squares below. When your answers are correct, all columns and rows will add to the same number.

A. PRETEND
B. CURTAINS
C. MONEY
D. SPEECH
E. GRANDPA
F. NORTH
G. SELL
H. NATHANIEL
I. CRANE
J. NEWSPAPERS
K. REYNOLDS
L. THOMAS
M. ORPHAN
N. HARRISON
O. GREENWOOD
P. ELEVATOR

1. Richard had to go to an ____'s home when his mother became ill
2. 'It symbolized to me all I had not felt and seen....'
3. Richard's father
4. Uncle Clark & Aunt Jody lived there
5. Richard threatened him with razors
6. Richard took part in a scheme that skimmed ____ from ticket sales
7. Richard and Harrison agreed to ____ to fight
8. Richard sold 'anti-Negro' ____
9. Threatened Richard & forced him to leave his good job
10. Richard refused to deliver the prewritten graduation ____
11. Little Richard set these on fire
12. Good-hearted white employer at optical company
13. Agrees to fight Richard for money
14. A Civil War veteran
15. Richard tried to ____ Bessie
16. Shorty operated one

A=	B=	C=	D=
E=	F=	G=	H=
I=	J=	K=	L=
M=	N=	O=	P=

22
Copyrighted

Black Boy Magic Squares 1 Answer Key

Match the definition with the vocabulary word. Put your answers in the magic squares below. When your answers are correct, all columns and rows will add to the same number.

A. PRETEND
B. CURTAINS
C. MONEY
D. SPEECH
E. GRANDPA
F. NORTH
G. SELL
H. NATHANIEL
I. CRANE
J. NEWSPAPERS
K. REYNOLDS
L. THOMAS
M. ORPHAN
N. HARRISON
O. GREENWOOD
P. ELEVATOR

1. Richard had to go to an ____'s home when his mother became ill
2. 'It symbolized to me all I had not felt and seen....'
3. Richard's father
4. Uncle Clark & Aunt Jody lived there
5. Richard threatened him with razors
6. Richard took part in a scheme that skimmed ____ from ticket sales
7. Richard and Harrison agreed to ____ to fight
8. Richard sold 'anti-Negro' ____
9. Threatened Richard & forced him to leave his good job
10. Richard refused to deliver the prewritten graduation ____
11. Little Richard set these on fire
12. Good-hearted white employer at optical company
13. Agrees to fight Richard for money
14. A Civil War veteran
15. Richard tried to ____ Bessie
16. Shorty operated one

A=7	B=11	C=6	D=10
E=14	F=2	G=15	H=3
I=12	J=8	K=9	L=5
M=1	N=13	O=4	P=16

Black Boy Magic Squares 2

Match the definition with the vocabulary word. Put your answers in the magic squares below. When your answers are correct, all columns and rows will add to the same number.

A. NORTH
B. CRANE
C. MOSS
D. DEATH
E. REYNOLDS
F. SHOT
G. GRIGGS
H. GRANNY
I. HARRISON
J. MARRY
K. GRANDPA
L. KNIFE
M. SOLDIERS
N. HELENA
O. COUNT
P. ALLY

1. Landlady in Memphis
2. Mrs. Moss wanted Bess to ____ Richard
3. White men ____ Uncle Hoskins
4. The coal man taught Richard to ____
5. Aunt Addie was Granny's ____
6. Threatened Richard & forced him to leave his good job
7. Agrees to fight Richard for money
8. 'The penalty of ____ awaited me if I make a false move...'
9. Richard saw these & prisoners when returning to Granny's
10. Strict Seventh-Day Adventist with whom Richard often lives
11. Richard defended himself against Aunt Addie with one
12. 'It symbolized to me all I had not felt and seen....'
13. Good-hearted white employer at optical company
14. A Civil War veteran
15. Richard's classmate who gives him advice
16. Wrights had to move from West ____

A=	B=	C=	D=
E=	F=	G=	H=
I=	J=	K=	L=
M=	N=	O=	P=

Black Boy Magic Squares 2 Answer Key

Match the definition with the vocabulary word. Put your answers in the magic squares below. When your answers are correct, all columns and rows will add to the same number.

A. NORTH
B. CRANE
C. MOSS
D. DEATH
E. REYNOLDS
F. SHOT
G. GRIGGS
H. GRANNY
I. HARRISON
J. MARRY
K. GRANDPA
L. KNIFE
M. SOLDIERS
N. HELENA
O. COUNT
P. ALLY

1. Landlady in Memphis
2. Mrs. Moss wanted Bess to ____ Richard
3. White men ____ Uncle Hoskins
4. The coal man taught Richard to ____
5. Aunt Addie was Granny's ____
6. Threatened Richard & forced him to leave his good job
7. Agrees to fight Richard for money
8. 'The penalty of ____ awaited me if I make a false move...'
9. Richard saw these & prisoners when returning to Granny's
10. Strict Seventh-Day Adventist with whom Richard often lives
11. Richard defended himself against Aunt Addie with one
12. 'It symbolized to me all I had not felt and seen....'
13. Good-hearted white employer at optical company
14. A Civil War veteran
15. Richard's classmate who gives him advice
16. Wrights had to move from West ____

A=12	B=13	C=1	D=8
E=6	F=3	G=15	H=10
I=7	J=2	K=14	L=11
M=9	N=16	O=4	P=5

Black Boy Magic Squares 3

Match the definition with the vocabulary word. Put your answers in the magic squares below. When your answers are correct, all columns and rows will add to the same number.

A. GRIGGS
B. GRANNY
C. CRANE
D. MAGGIE
E. NEWSPAPERS
F. BAPTIZED
G. SHOT
H. CLARK
I. OLIN
J. MONEY
K. KITTEN
L. ELEVATOR
M. CURTAINS
N. SHORTY
O. NATHANIEL
P. AUNT

1. Takes Richard to live in Greenwood
2. Richard's classmate who gives him advice
3. Strict Seventh-Day Adventist with whom Richard often lives
4. White men ____ Uncle Hoskins
5. Richard took part in a scheme that skimmed ____ from ticket sales
6. Richard's father
7. Addie or Maggie to Richard
8. Set up fight between Richard and Harrison
9. Richard hanged it to get back at his father
10. Elevator operator
11. Little Richard set these on fire
12. Shorty operated one
13. Richard sold 'anti-Negro' ____
14. Richard's favorite aunt
15. Good-hearted white employer at optical company
16. Richard agreed to be ____ into the church to please his mother

A=	B=	C=	D=
E=	F=	G=	H=
I=	J=	K=	L=
M=	N=	O=	P=

Black Boy Magic Squares 3 Answer Key

Match the definition with the vocabulary word. Put your answers in the magic squares below. When your answers are correct, all columns and rows will add to the same number.

- A. GRIGGS
- B. GRANNY
- C. CRANE
- D. MAGGIE
- E. NEWSPAPERS
- F. BAPTIZED
- G. SHOT
- H. CLARK
- I. OLIN
- J. MONEY
- K. KITTEN
- L. ELEVATOR
- M. CURTAINS
- N. SHORTY
- O. NATHANIEL
- P. AUNT

1. Takes Richard to live in Greenwood
2. Richard's classmate who gives him advice
3. Strict Seventh-Day Adventist with whom Richard often lives
4. White men _____ Uncle Hoskins
5. Richard took part in a scheme that skimmed _____ from ticket sales
6. Richard's father
7. Addie or Maggie to Richard
8. Set up fight between Richard and Harrison
9. Richard hanged it to get back at his father
10. Elevator operator
11. Little Richard set these on fire
12. Shorty operated one
13. Richard sold 'anti-Negro' _____
14. Richard's favorite aunt
15. Good-hearted white employer at optical company
16. Richard agreed to be _____ into the church to please his mother

A=2	B=3	C=15	D=14
E=13	F=16	G=4	H=1
I=8	J=5	K=9	L=12
M=11	N=10	O=6	P=7

Black Boy Magic Squares 4

Match the definition with the vocabulary word. Put your answers in the magic squares below. When your answers are correct, all columns and rows will add to the same number.

A. REYNOLDS
B. SIMON
C. KNIFE
D. GRANDPA
E. GRANNY
F. HELENA

G. HARRISON
H. SHORTY
I. SHOT
J. SOLDIERS
K. SPEECH
L. SELL

M. NEWSPAPERS
N. ELEVATOR
O. CLARK
P. INSURANCE

1. Wrights had to move from West ____
2. White men ____ Uncle Hoskins
3. Takes Richard to live in Greenwood
4. A Civil War veteran
5. Richard sold 'anti-Negro' ____
6. Head of the orphanage
7. Elevator operator
8. Richard refused to deliver the prewritten graduation ____
9. Richard defended himself against Aunt Addie with one
10. Brother Manse's work
11. Richard saw these & prisoners when returning to Granny's
12. Strict Seventh-Day Adventist with whom Richard often lives
13. Richard tried to ____ Bessie
14. Agrees to fight Richard for money
15. Threatened Richard & forced him to leave his good job
16. Shorty operated one

A=	B=	C=	D=
E=	F=	G=	H=
I=	J=	K=	L=
M=	N=	O=	P=

Black Boy Magic Squares 4 Answer Key

Match the definition with the vocabulary word. Put your answers in the magic squares below. When your answers are correct, all columns and rows will add to the same number.

A. REYNOLDS
B. SIMON
C. KNIFE
D. GRANDPA
E. GRANNY
F. HELENA
G. HARRISON
H. SHORTY
I. SHOT
J. SOLDIERS
K. SPEECH
L. SELL
M. NEWSPAPERS
N. ELEVATOR
O. CLARK
P. INSURANCE

1. Wrights had to move from West ____
2. White men ____ Uncle Hoskins
3. Takes Richard to live in Greenwood
4. A Civil War veteran
5. Richard sold 'anti-Negro' ____
6. Head of the orphanage
7. Elevator operator
8. Richard refused to deliver the prewritten graduation ____
9. Richard defended himself against Aunt Addie with one
10. Brother Manse's work
11. Richard saw these & prisoners when returning to Granny's
12. Strict Seventh-Day Adventist with whom Richard often lives
13. Richard tried to ____ Bessie
14. Agrees to fight Richard for money
15. Threatened Richard & forced him to leave his good job
16. Shorty operated one

A=15	B=6	C=9	D=4
E=12	F=1	G=14	H=7
I=2	J=11	K=8	L=13
M=5	N=16	O=3	P=10

Black Boy Word Search 1

```
O V K X C C W H C E E P S R C A D G
C L G K L R H E A G Z R R W X D E V
W C I D A T T L D R G H I E R D A V
S R S N R K E E M A R R Y C T I T L
O H I O K L I N M N I I K S H E H Z
L L N G L D G A B N G E S V I A N D
D E F A H V G H L Y G M C O A M R D
I I U G V T A F J D S O D C N E O D
E N L S R O M Y U V U Z S U G M G N
R A S S E L O J R N C B T R E P S T
S H M U Y L Q D T A T K E T L H T P
L T Z A R M L Z O S Z Y T A K I A F
K A U N N A B D W O N O B I P S L S
K N I H T M N O E O H Y R N S K L Q
T K I T T E N C L S B E S S L N Y W
N D Y F K Y M D E R R P O A D K W Q
C R A N E B S N H Y K M F M O N E Y
P Q T R D S P W Q B J R T Y H Y X Z
```

'It symbolized to me all I had not felt and seen....' (5)
'My mother's suffering grew into a ____ in my mind....' (6)
'The ____ of Hell's Half-Acre' (6)
'The penalty of ____ awaited me if I make a false move...' (5)
A boy had ____ in Richard's bed at Uncle Clark's house (4)
Addie or Maggie to Richard (4)
Advice Griggs gave Richard (5)
Agrees to fight Richard for money (8)
Aunt Addie was Granny's____ (4)
Author's last name (6)
Black boy is about him (7)
Brother Manse's work (9)
Good-hearted white employer at optical company (5)
Granny hit Richard with one when he told her to 'kiss back there' (5)
Granny thought story books were ____ (6)
Granny's ally; Richard's teacher (5)
Head of the orphanage (5)
Helped Richard get library books (4)
Home town of Mrs. Moss and Bess (7)
If Richard had seen an ____ like Jacob had, he would have believed, too (5)
Landlady in Memphis (4)
Little Richard set these on fire (8)
Mrs. Moss wanted Bess to ____ Richard (5)

Richard and Harrison agreed to ____ to fight (7)
Richard defended himself against Aunt Addie with one (5)
Richard hanged it to get back at his father (6)
Richard refused to deliver the prewritten graduation ____ (6)
Richard saw these & prisoners when returning to Granny's (8)
Richard threatened to cut Uncle Tom with ____ (6)
Richard took part in a scheme that skimmed ____ from ticket sales (5)
Richard tried to ____ Bessie (4)
Richard's classmate who gives him advice (6)
Richard's father (9)
Richard's favorite aunt (6)
Richard's mother (4)
Ruled in Richard's father's favor in court (5)
Set up fight between Richard and Harrison (4)
Strict Seventh-Day Adventist with whom Richard often lives (6)
Takes Richard to live in Greenwood (5)
The coal man taught Richard to ____ (5)
Threatened Richard & forced him to leave his good job (8)
White men ____ Uncle Hoskins (4)
Willing to marry Richard (4)
Wrights had to move from West ____ (6)

Black Boy Word Search 1 Answer Key

'It symbolized to me all I had not felt and seen....' (5)
'My mother's suffering grew into a ____ in my mind....' (6)
'The ____ of Hell's Half-Acre' (6)
'The penalty of ____ awaited me if I make a false move...' (5)
A boy had ____ in Richard's bed at Uncle Clark's house (4)
Addie or Maggie to Richard (4)
Advice Griggs gave Richard (5)
Agrees to fight Richard for money (8)
Aunt Addie was Granny's ____ (4)
Author's last name (6)
Black boy is about him (7)
Brother Manse's work (9)
Good-hearted white employer at optical company (5)
Granny hit Richard with one when he told her to 'kiss back there' (5)
Granny thought story books were ____ (6)
Granny's ally; Richard's teacher (5)
Head of the orphanage (5)
Helped Richard get library books (4)
Home town of Mrs. Moss and Bess (7)
If Richard had seen an ____ like Jacob had, he would have believed, too (5)
Landlady in Memphis (4)
Little Richard set these on fire (8)
Mrs. Moss wanted Bess to ____ Richard (5)
Richard and Harrison agreed to ____ to fight (7)
Richard defended himself against Aunt Addie with one (5)
Richard hanged it to get back at his father (6)
Richard refused to deliver the prewritten graduation ____ (6)
Richard saw these & prisoners when returning to Granny's (8)
Richard threatened to cut Uncle Tom with ____ (6)
Richard took part in a scheme that skimmed ____ from ticket sales (5)
Richard tried to ____ Bessie (4)
Richard's classmate who gives him advice (6)
Richard's father (9)
Richard's favorite aunt (6)
Richard's mother (4)
Ruled in Richard's father's favor in court (5)
Set up fight between Richard and Harrison (4)
Strict Seventh-Day Adventist with whom Richard often lives (6)
Takes Richard to live in Greenwood (5)
The coal man taught Richard to ____ (5)
Threatened Richard & forced him to leave his good job (8)
White men ____ Uncle Hoskins (4)
Willing to marry Richard (4)
Wrights had to move from West ____ (6)

Black Boy Word Search 2

```
M O S S H S R G S V O O D O O N D B
L U F N I S I V W Y G X Y G J S K J
K J C P H T K M K P M J E J D B A Z
G I N O O L A S O K I B N L K P N K
M H T H I N K S K N I L O J U D G E
T A T T C W R R S I V N M L R R E A
V R S D E O G U N F Y N R Z A F L Z
Q R E P Z N R M G E T Q J N B L L S
N I V A E A M E R I N G D N E N E Y
D S R Y N E W M A G U P N E V O S Y
T O G C T G C P N G A F E W A R N D
A N E P O R M H N A T S T S L T A J
B D N W W I H I Y M H C E P L H H Z
D E D L E G N S Y O O L R A Y E P C
C P S I L G Z R R U M A P P G L R T
R H R S E S R T N Y A R H E Q E O G
F A L K H A Y T X X S K C R A N E V
Y Y K K M W R I G H T B M S K A B V
```

'It symbolized to me all I had not felt and seen....' (5)
'My mother's suffering grew into a ____ in my mind....' (6)
'The ____ of Hell's Half-Acre' (6)
'The penalty of ____ awaited me if I make a false move...' (5)
A Civil War veteran (7)
A boy had ____ in Richard's bed at Uncle Clark's house (4)
Addie or Maggie to Richard (4)
Advice Griggs gave Richard (5)
Agrees to fight Richard for money (8)
Aunt Addie was Granny's____ (4)
Author's last name (6)
Brother Manse's work (9)
Elevator operator (6)
Good-hearted white employer at optical company (5)
Granny hit Richard with one when he told her to 'kiss back there' (5)
Granny thought story books were ____ (6)
Granny's ally; Richard's teacher (5)
Head of the orphanage (5)
Helped Richard get library books (4)
Home town of Mrs. Moss and Bess (7)
If Richard had seen an ____ like Jacob had, he would have believed, too (5)
Landlady in Memphis (4)
Mrs. Moss wanted Bess to ____ Richard (5)

Place where Richard passed time at age 6 (6)
Richard and Harrison agreed to ____ to fight (7)
Richard defended himself against Aunt Addie with one (5)
Richard had to go to an ____'s home when his mother became ill (6)
Richard hanged it to get back at his father (6)
Richard refused to deliver the prewritten graduation ____ (6)
Richard sold 'anti-Negro' ____ (10)
Richard threatened him with razors (6)
Richard threatened to cut Uncle Tom with ____ (6)
Richard took part in a scheme that skimmed ____ from ticket sales (5)
Richard tried to ____ Bessie (4)
Richard's classmate who gives him advice (6)
Richard's favorite aunt (6)
Richard's mother (4)
Ruled in Richard's father's favor in court (5)
Set up fight between Richard and Harrison (4)
Strict Seventh-Day Adventist with whom Richard often lives (6)
Takes Richard to live in Greenwood (5)
The coal man taught Richard to ____ (5)
Threatened Richard & forced him to leave his good job (8)
White men ____ Uncle Hoskins (4)
Willing to marry Richard (4)
Wrights had to move from West ____ (6)

Black Boy Word Search 2 Answer Key

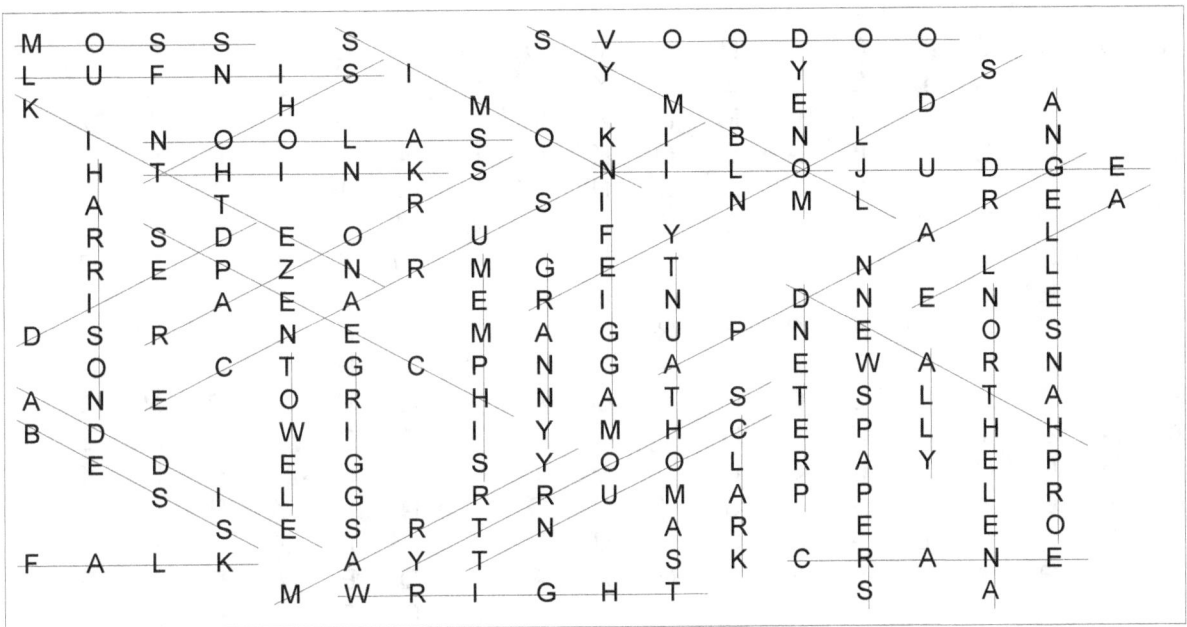

'It symbolized to me all I had not felt and seen....' (5)
'My mother's suffering grew into a ____ in my mind....' (6)
'The ____ of Hell's Half-Acre' (6)
'The penalty of ____ awaited me if I make a false move...' (5)
A Civil War veteran (7)
A boy had ____ in Richard's bed at Uncle Clark's house (4)
Addie or Maggie to Richard (4)
Advice Griggs gave Richard (5)
Agrees to fight Richard for money (8)
Aunt Addie was Granny's ____ (4)
Author's last name (6)
Brother Manse's work (9)
Elevator operator (6)
Good-hearted white employer at optical company (5)
Granny hit Richard with one when he told her to 'kiss back there' (5)
Granny thought story books were ____ (6)
Granny's ally; Richard's teacher (5)
Head of the orphanage (5)
Helped Richard get library books (4)
Home town of Mrs. Moss and Bess (7)
If Richard had seen an ____ like Jacob had, he would have believed, too (5)
Landlady in Memphis (4)
Mrs. Moss wanted Bess to ____ Richard (5)

Place where Richard passed time at age 6 (6)
Richard and Harrison agreed to ____ to fight (7)
Richard defended himself against Aunt Addie with one (5)
Richard had to go to an ____'s home when his mother became ill (6)
Richard hanged it to get back at his father (6)
Richard refused to deliver the prewritten graduation ____ (6)
Richard sold 'anti-Negro' ____ (10)
Richard threatened him with razors (6)
Richard threatened to cut Uncle Tom with ____ (6)
Richard took part in a scheme that skimmed ____ from ticket sales (5)
Richard tried to ____ Bessie (4)
Richard's classmate who gives him advice (6)
Richard's favorite aunt (6)
Richard's mother (4)
Ruled in Richard's father's favor in court (5)
Set up fight between Richard and Harrison (4)
Strict Seventh-Day Adventist with whom Richard often lives (6)
Takes Richard to live in Greenwood (5)
The coal man taught Richard to ____ (5)
Threatened Richard & forced him to leave his good job (8)
White men ____ Uncle Hoskins (4)
Willing to marry Richard (4)
Wrights had to move from West ____ (6)

Black Boy Word Search 3

```
M O S S D S F N S V O O D O O V B R
L U F N I S I B L Y F Q Y K D S G Y
K K B M H P L M N Z M J E G D X A J
T I N O O L A S O K I B N L S D N X
W H T H I N K S S N I L O J U D G E
B A R T J N R D S I T N M L G R E A
L R S D E O Z U Q F Y K W B A S L R
Q R E P Z N R M G E T S C N P L L P
V I T A E A C E R I N P D N E N E G
D S R G N E L M A G U P N E S O S P
Z O R C T G C P N G A W E W A R N D
A N E J O R T H N A T S T S L T A B
B D L H W I Q I Y M H C E P L H H X
D E D K E G H S Y O O L R A Y E P G
C P S I L G J R N U M A P P F L R B
B T R S E S R T N X A R Q E Y E O G
F A L K V A Y T J K S K C R A N E V
H P Z S M W R I G H T H T S J A V J
```

ADDIE	GRANDPA	MONEY	SHOT
ALLY	GRANNY	MOSS	SIMON
ANGEL	GRIGGS	NEWSPAPERS	SINFUL
AUNT	HARRISON	NORTH	SPEECH
BESS	HELENA	OLIN	SYMBOL
CLARK	INSURANCE	ORPHAN	THINK
COUNT	JUDGE	PRETEND	THOMAS
CRANE	KITTEN	RAZORS	TOWEL
DEATH	KNIFE	REYNOLDS	VOODOO
DIED	MAGGIE	SALOON	WRIGHT
ELLA	MARRY	SELL	
FALK	MEMPHIS	SHORTY	

Black Boy Word Search 3 Answer Key

```
M  O  S  S     S           S  V  O  O  D  O  O
L  U  F  N  I  S        Y     M     Y     D     S
K        H     I     M        E        D        A
      N  O  O  L  A  S  O  K  I  B  N  L        N
      T  H  I  N  K  S     N  I  L  O  J  U  D  G  E
H     T     R        S  I  N  M     L     R     E  A
A     S  D  E  O     U     F     Y     N     A     L
R     E  P  Z  N  R  M  G  E  T        N     L     L
R        A  E  A  E  M  R  I  N     D  N  E  N     E
I  D  S  R     N  C  P  A  G  U  P  N  E     O  S
S     O     T  E     H  M  A  T     E  T  W  R  N
O     N  E  O  R  C  I  N  H  S  T  E  S  A  T  A
N  A     D  W  I     S  Y  O  C  E  R  P  L  H  H
B        E  E  G  H  R  R  N  L  R  P  A  Y  E  P
  E      D  L  G  I  Y     U  A  A  P  E     L  R
          S  E  S  S  R  T     M     P     L  E  O
F  A  L  K     A  Y  T        S  K  C  R  A  N  E
            M  W  R  I  G  H  T        S        A
```

ADDIE	GRANDPA	MONEY	SHOT
ALLY	GRANNY	MOSS	SIMON
ANGEL	GRIGGS	NEWSPAPERS	SINFUL
AUNT	HARRISON	NORTH	SPEECH
BESS	HELENA	OLIN	SYMBOL
CLARK	INSURANCE	ORPHAN	THINK
COUNT	JUDGE	PRETEND	THOMAS
CRANE	KITTEN	RAZORS	TOWEL
DEATH	KNIFE	REYNOLDS	VOODOO
DIED	MAGGIE	SALOON	WRIGHT
ELLA	MARRY	SELL	
FALK	MEMPHIS	SHORTY	

Black Boy Word Search 4

```
K G R A N D P A J E Z S B E S S P D
D I S P E E C H I S Y R I C H A R D
I G T G R I G G S M R A Z O R T E Z
N R S T K K G J B M L S F Q T K T G
S A R B E A F O C A B H C M N G E F
U N E H M N L R U R P O T L U S N N
R N I H L Y L F R R V T K L A F D A
A Y D X T H O B T Y H O I M J R N N
N T L R W Q T L A G W S O Z T G K V
C N O R T H D E I D P H E D E A T H
E H S W I H C R N N T I F L O D M T
S A X N E E W O S R D Q I C L O O H
J R K E M L J R D E B N Q L N S S Y
P R M K C E U P A L L Y K U O E S M
D I O C R N D H B D L V F O N I X W
M S N N G A G A R J A N L A M N H T
B O E E D Z E N C N I A R O L X M W
Y N Y M E M P H I S S C N C O U N T
```

ADDIE	FALK	MENCKEN	SIMON
ALLY	GRANDPA	MONEY	SINFUL
ANGEL	GRANNY	MOSS	SOLDIERS
AUNT	GRIGGS	NORTH	SPEECH
BAPTIZED	HARRISON	OLIN	SYMBOL
BESS	HELENA	ORPHAN	THINK
CLARK	INSURANCE	PRETEND	THOMAS
COUNT	JUDGE	RAZORS	TOWEL
CRANE	KITTEN	RICHARD	VOODOO
CURTAINS	KNIFE	SALOON	WRIGHT
DEATH	MAGGIE	SELL	
DIED	MARRY	SHORTY	
ELLA	MEMPHIS	SHOT	

Black Boy Word Search 4 Answer Key

ADDIE	FALK	MENCKEN	SIMON
ALLY	GRANDPA	MONEY	SINFUL
ANGEL	GRANNY	MOSS	SOLDIERS
AUNT	GRIGGS	NORTH	SPEECH
BAPTIZED	HARRISON	OLIN	SYMBOL
BESS	HELENA	ORPHAN	THINK
CLARK	INSURANCE	PRETEND	THOMAS
COUNT	JUDGE	RAZORS	TOWEL
CRANE	KITTEN	RICHARD	VOODOO
CURTAINS	KNIFE	SALOON	WRIGHT
DEATH	MAGGIE	SELL	
DIED	MARRY	SHORTY	
ELLA	MEMPHIS	SHOT	

Black Boy Crossword 1

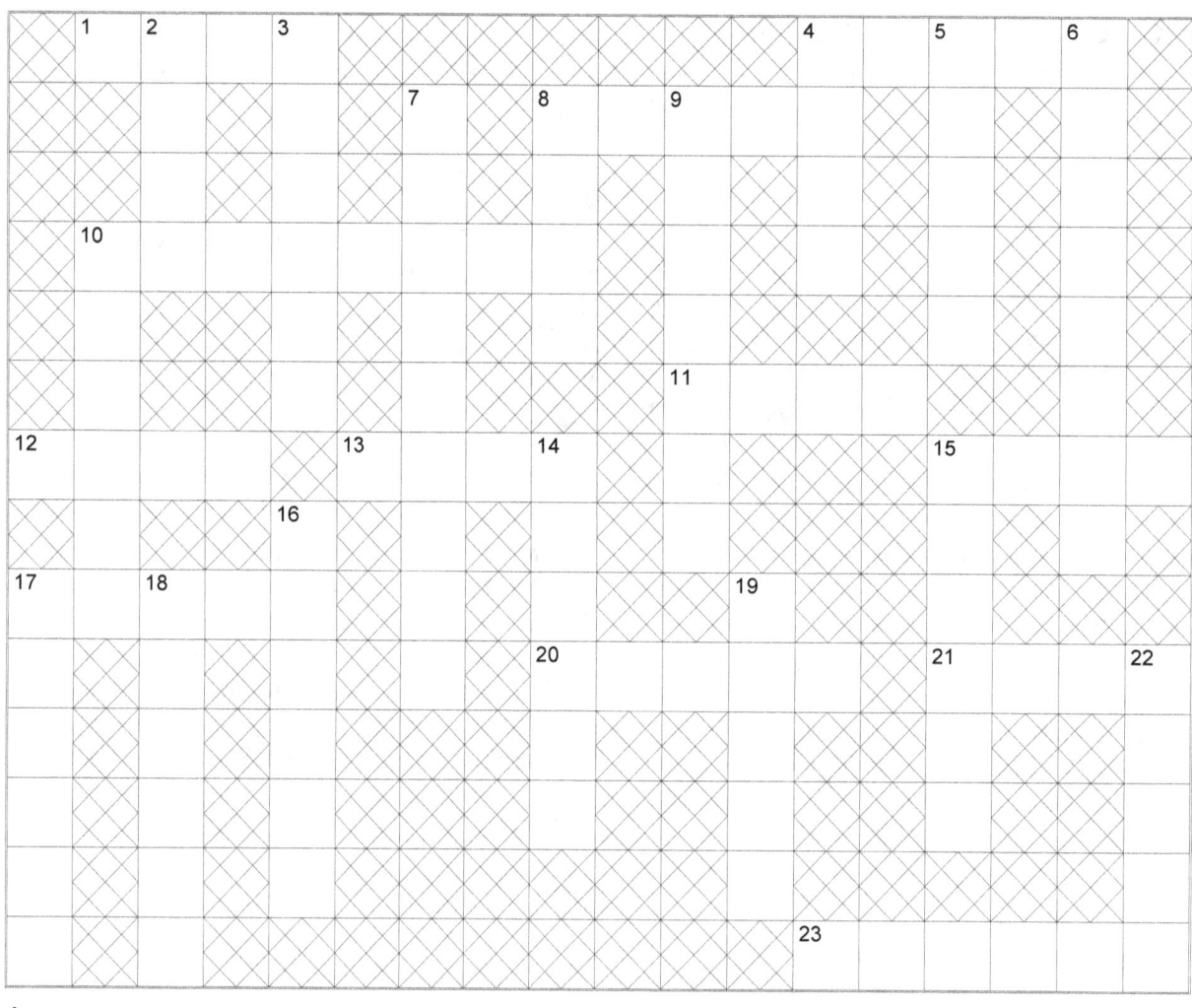

Across
1. Willing to marry Richard
4. Granny's ally; Richard's teacher
8. If Richard had seen an ____ like Jacob had, he would have believed, too
10. Agrees to fight Richard for money
11. A boy had ____ in Richard's bed at Uncle Clark's house
12. Richard tried to ____ Bessie
13. Helped Richard get library books
15. White men ____ Uncle Hoskins
17. Mrs. Moss wanted Bess to ____ Richard
20. Advice Griggs gave Richard
21. Set up fight between Richard and Harrison
23. Richard refused to deliver the prewritten graduation ____

Down
2. Richard's mother
3. Elevator operator
4. Aunt Addie was Granny's____
5. 'The penalty of ____ awaited me if I make a false move...'
6. Shorty operated one
7. Brother Manse's work
8. Addie or Maggie to Richard
9. A Civil War veteran
10. Wrights had to move from West ____
14. Richard hanged it to get back at his father
15. Place where Richard passed time at age 6
16. 'My mother's suffering grew into a ____ in my mind....'
17. Richard's favorite aunt
18. Richard threatened to cut Uncle Tom with ____
19. Richard defended himself against Aunt Addie with one
22. 'It symbolized to me all I had not felt and seen....'

Black Boy Crossword 1 Answer Key

	1 B	2 E	3 S					4 A	5 D	6 E	
		L		H		7 I	8 A	N	G	E	L
		L		O		N	U	R	L	A	E
	10 H	A	R	R	I	S	O	N	A	Y	T	V
		E		T		U		T	N		H	A
		L		Y		R			11 D	I	E	D	T
12 S	E	L	L		13 F	A	L	14 K	P		15 S	H	O	T
	N			16 S	N		I	A		A	R	
17 M	18 A	R	R	Y		C	E	T		19 K		L	
A	A		M			E	20 T	H	I	N	K	21 O	L	22 I	N
G	Z		B				E			I		O		N
G	O		O				N			F		N		O
I	R		L							E				R
E	S									23 S	P	E	E	C	H

Across

1. Willing to marry Richard
4. Granny's ally; Richard's teacher
8. If Richard had seen an ____ like Jacob had, he would have believed, too
10. Agrees to fight Richard for money
11. A boy had ____ in Richard's bed at Uncle Clark's house
12. Richard tried to ____ Bessie
13. Helped Richard get library books
15. White men ____ Uncle Hoskins
17. Mrs. Moss wanted Bess to ____ Richard
20. Advice Griggs gave Richard
21. Set up fight between Richard and Harrison
23. Richard refused to deliver the prewritten graduation ____

Down

2. Richard's mother
3. Elevator operator
4. Aunt Addie was Granny's ____
5. 'The penalty of ____ awaited me if I make a false move...'
6. Shorty operated one
7. Brother Manse's work
8. Addie or Maggie to Richard
9. A Civil War veteran
10. Wrights had to move from West ____
14. Richard hanged it to get back at his father
15. Place where Richard passed time at age 6
16. 'My mother's suffering grew into a ____ in my mind....'
17. Richard's favorite aunt
18. Richard threatened to cut Uncle Tom with ____
19. Richard defended himself against Aunt Addie with one
22. 'It symbolized to me all I had not felt and seen....'

Black Boy Crossword 2

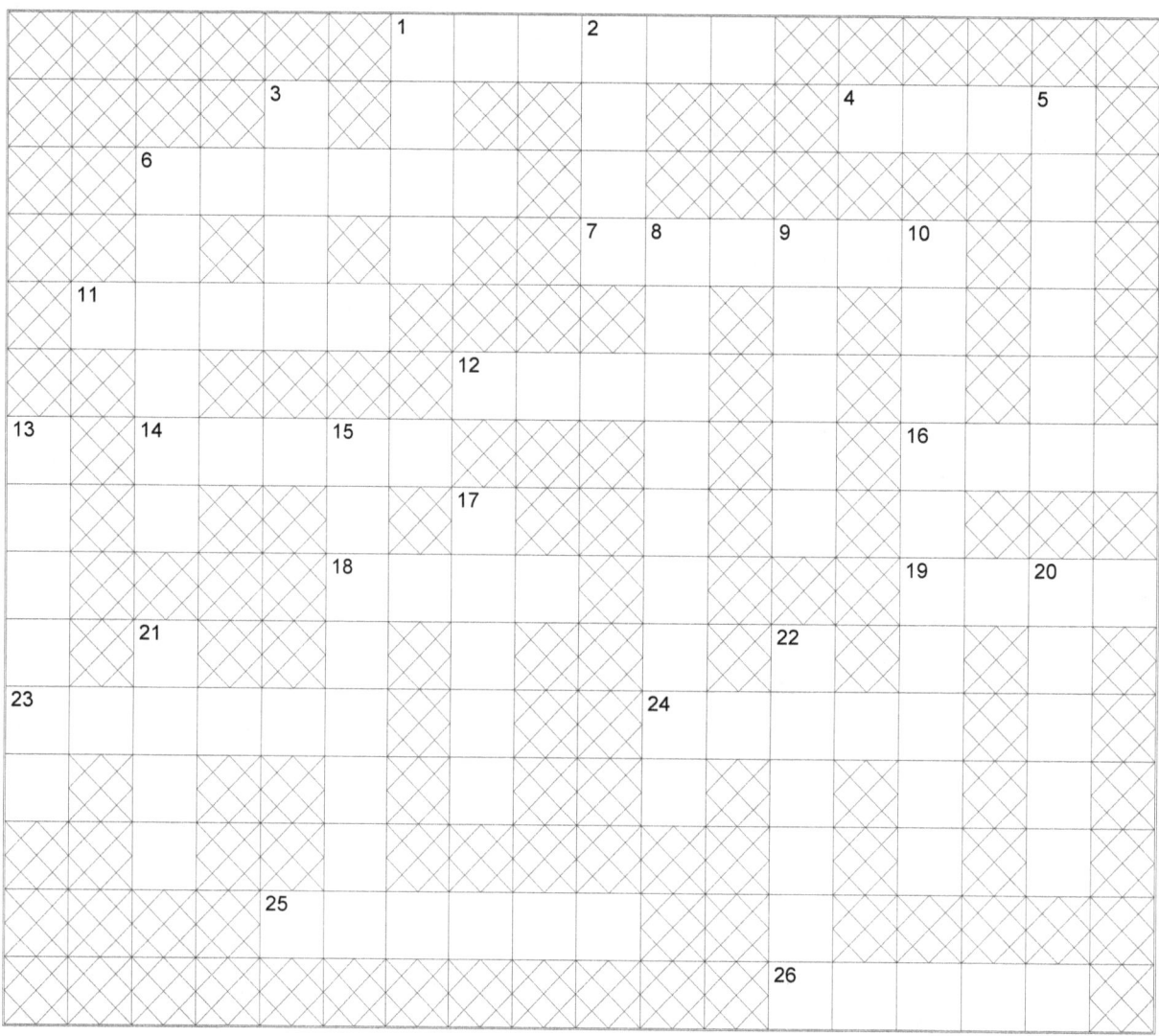

Across
1. Granny thought story books were ____
4. Landlady in Memphis
6. Place where Richard passed time at age 6
7. Richard hanged it to get back at his father
11. The coal man taught Richard to ____
12. Willing to marry Richard
14. Granny hit Richard with one when he told her to 'kiss back there'
16. Richard tried to ____ Bessie
18. Richard's mother
19. Addie or Maggie to Richard
23. Wrights had to move from West ____
24. Good-hearted white employer at optical company
25. Richard's classmate who gives him advice
26. Head of the orphanage

Down
1. White men ____ Uncle Hoskins
2. Helped Richard get library books
3. Set up fight between Richard and Harrison
5. 'My mother's suffering grew into a ____ in my mind....'
6. Elevator operator
8. Brother Manse's work
9. Advice Griggs gave Richard
10. Richard sold 'anti-Negro' ____
13. Author's last name
15. Shorty operated one
17. Takes Richard to live in Greenwood
20. 'It symbolized to me all I had not felt and seen....'
21. Aunt Addie was Granny's____
22. Richard threatened to cut Uncle Tom with ____

Black Boy Crossword 2 Answer Key

					¹S	I	²N	F	U	L				
		³O		H			A				⁴M	O	S	⁵S
	⁶S	A	L	O	O	N		L						Y
		H		I		T			⁷K	⁸I	T	⁹T	¹⁰E	N	M
	¹¹C	O	U	N	T					N		H	E		B
		R				¹²B	E	S	S			I		W		O
¹³W		¹⁴T	O	¹⁵W	E	L			U			N		¹⁶S	E	L	L
R		Y		L			¹⁷C		R			K		P		
I				¹⁸E	L	L	A		A					¹⁹A	U	²⁰N	T
G		²¹A		V			A		N			²²R		P		O
²³H	E	L	E	N	A		R		²⁴C	R	A	N	E		R
T		L		T			K		E			Z		R		T
		Y		O								O		S		H
			²⁵G	R	I	G	G	S				R			
												²⁶S	I	M	O	N

Across
1. Granny thought story books were ____
4. Landlady in Memphis
6. Place where Richard passed time at age 6
7. Richard hanged it to get back at his father
11. The coal man taught Richard to ____
12. Willing to marry Richard
14. Granny hit Richard with one when he told her to 'kiss back there'
16. Richard tried to ____ Bessie
18. Richard's mother
19. Addie or Maggie to Richard
23. Wrights had to move from West ____
24. Good-hearted white employer at optical company
25. Richard's classmate who gives him advice
26. Head of the orphanage

Down
1. White men ____ Uncle Hoskins
2. Helped Richard get library books
3. Set up fight between Richard and Harrison
5. 'My mother's suffering grew into a ____ in my mind....'
6. Elevator operator
8. Brother Manse's work
9. Advice Griggs gave Richard
10. Richard sold 'anti-Negro' ____
13. Author's last name
15. Shorty operated one
17. Takes Richard to live in Greenwood
20. 'It symbolized to me all I had not felt and seen....'
21. Aunt Addie was Granny's____
22. Richard threatened to cut Uncle Tom with ____

Black Boy Crossword 3

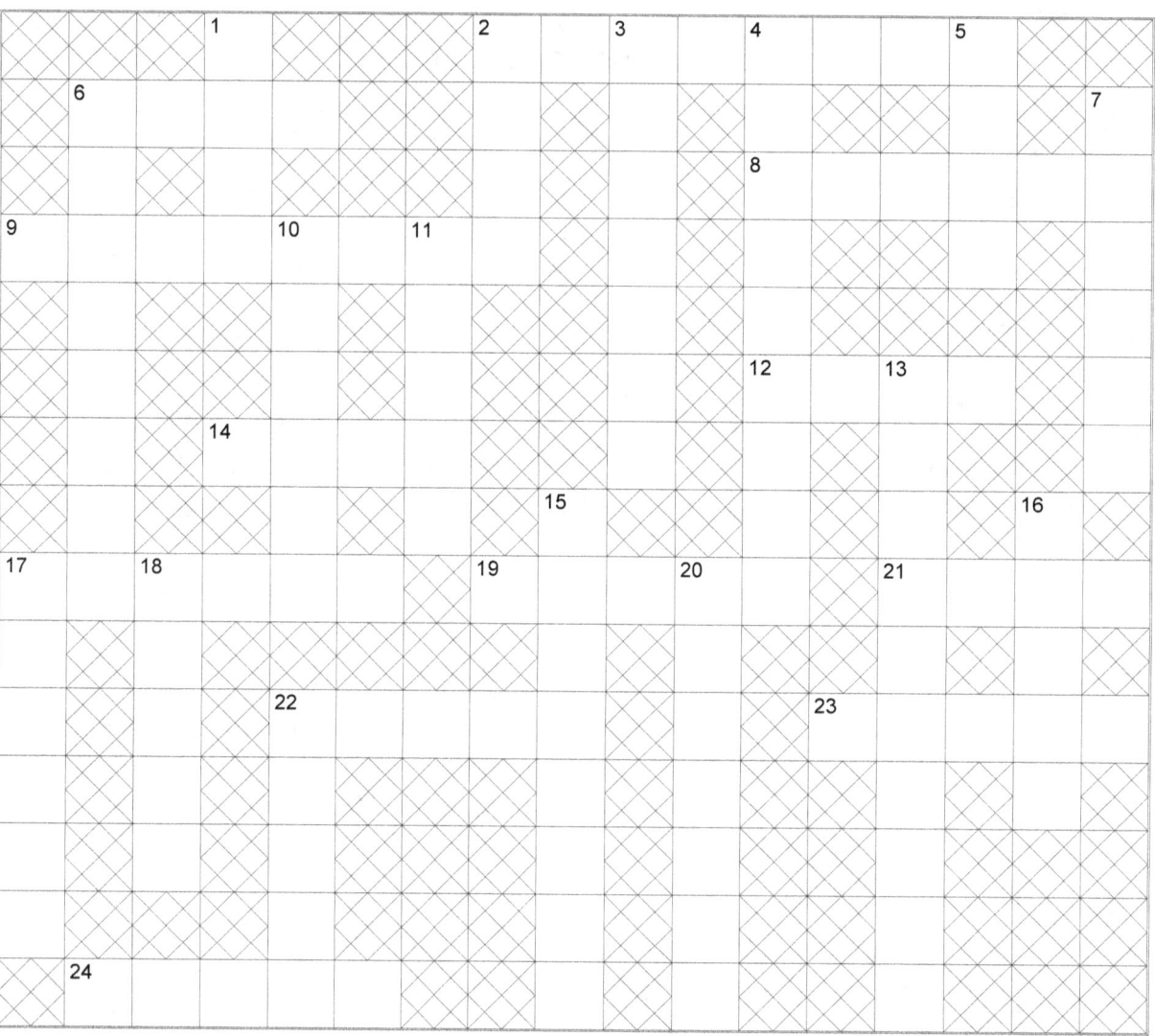

Across
2. Richard agreed to be ____ into the church to please his mother
6. Richard's mother
8. Richard refused to deliver the prewritten graduation ____
9. Threatened Richard & forced him to leave his good job
12. Addie or Maggie to Richard
14. White men ____ Uncle Hoskins
17. Strict Seventh-Day Adventist with whom Richard often lives
19. Ruled in Richard's father's favor in court
21. Richard tried to ____ Bessie
22. The coal man taught Richard to ____
23. Mrs. Moss wanted Bess to ____ Richard
24. Granny hit Richard with one when he told her to 'kiss back there'

Down
1. Set up fight between Richard and Harrison
2. Willing to marry Richard
3. Richard and Harrison agreed to ____ to fight
4. Brother Manse's work
5. A boy had ____ in Richard's bed at Uncle Clark's house
6. Shorty operated one
7. Elevator operator
10. Richard had to go to an ____'s home when his mother became ill
11. 'The penalty of ____ awaited me if I make a false move...'
13. Richard sold 'anti-Negro' ____
15. Little Richard set these on fire
16. Takes Richard to live in Greenwood
17. Richard's classmate who gives him advice
18. Granny's ally; Richard's teacher
20. A Civil War veteran
22. Good-hearted white employer at optical company

Black Boy Crossword 3 Answer Key

		1 O			2 B	A	3 P	T	4 I	Z	5 D		
	6 E	L	L	A			R		N		I		7 S
	L		I		E		E		8 S	P	E	E	C	H
9 R	E	Y	N	10 O	L	11 D	S		T		U		D		O
	V			R		E			E		R				R
	A			P		A			N		12 A	U	13 N	T	
	T		14 S	H	O	T			D		N		E		Y
	O			A		H		15 C			C		W		16 C
17 G	R	18 A	N	N	Y		19 J	U	D	20 G	E		21 S	E	L	L
R		D					R			R			P			A
I		D		22 C	O	U	N	T		A		23 M	A	R	R	Y
G		I		R			A			N		P			K	
G		E		A			I			D		E				
S				N			N			P		R				
	24 T	O	W	E	L		S			A		S				

Across
2. Richard agreed to be ____ into the church to please his mother
6. Richard's mother
8. Richard refused to deliver the prewritten graduation ____
9. Threatened Richard & forced him to leave his good job
12. Addie or Maggie to Richard
14. White men ____ Uncle Hoskins
17. Strict Seventh-Day Adventist with whom Richard often lives
19. Ruled in Richard's father's favor in court
21. Richard tried to ____ Bessie
22. The coal man taught Richard to ____
23. Mrs. Moss wanted Bess to ____ Richard
24. Granny hit Richard with one when he told her to 'kiss back there'

Down
1. Set up fight between Richard and Harrison
2. Willing to marry Richard
3. Richard and Harrison agreed to ____ to fight
4. Brother Manse's work
5. A boy had ____ in Richard's bed at Uncle Clark's house
6. Shorty operated one
7. Elevator operator
10. Richard had to go to an ____'s home when his mother became ill
11. 'The penalty of ____ awaited me if I make a false move...'
13. Richard sold 'anti-Negro' ____
15. Little Richard set these on fire
16. Takes Richard to live in Greenwood
17. Richard's classmate who gives him advice
18. Granny's ally; Richard's teacher
20. A Civil War veteran
22. Good-hearted white employer at optical company

Black Boy Crossword 4

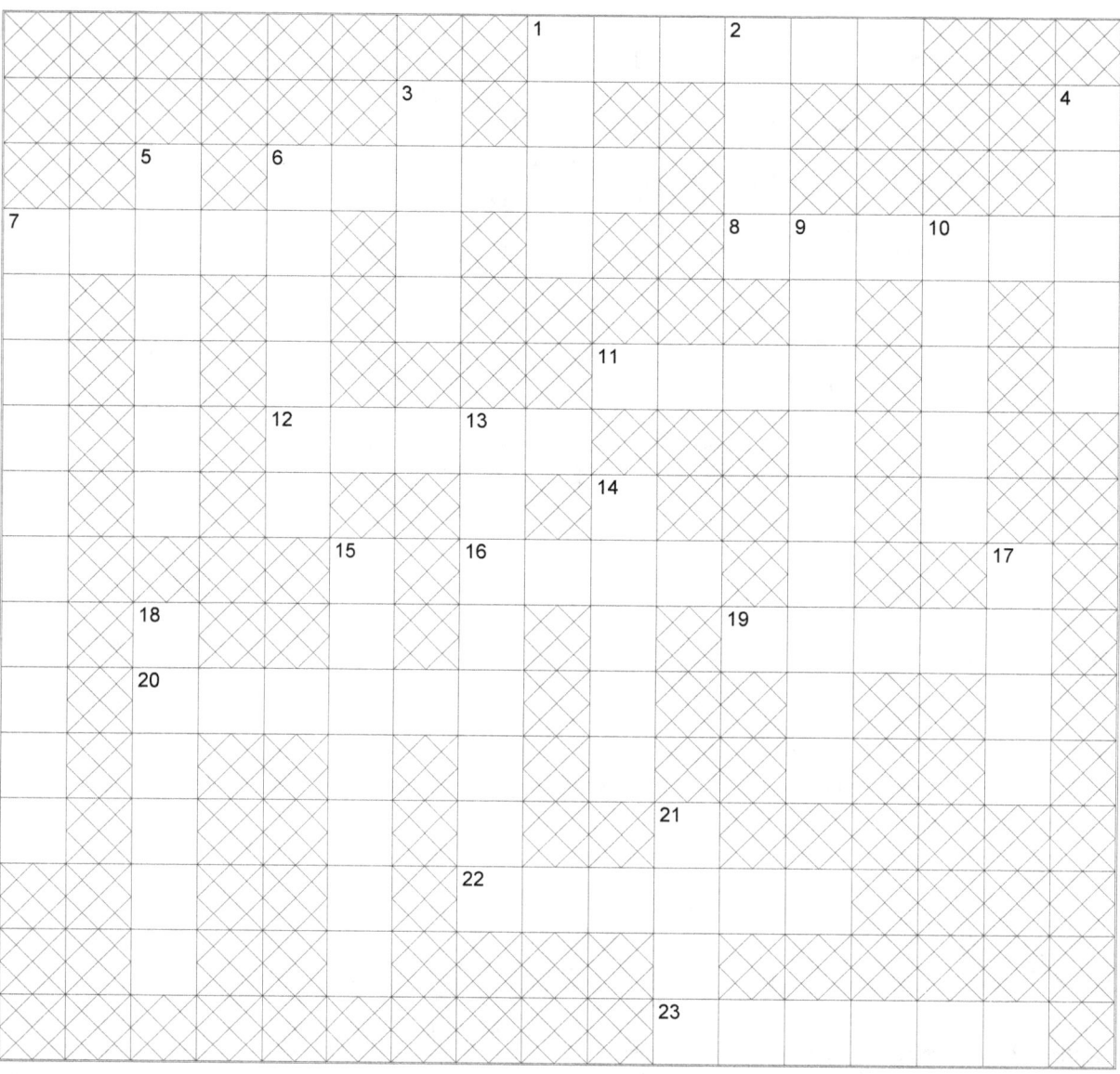

Across
1. Granny thought story books were ____
6. Place where Richard passed time at age 6
7. 'It symbolized to me all I had not felt and seen....'
8. Richard hanged it to get back at his father
11. Willing to marry Richard
12. Granny hit Richard with one when he told her to 'kiss back there'
16. Richard's mother
19. If Richard had seen an ____ like Jacob had, he would have believed, too
20. Wrights had to move from West ____
22. Richard threatened to cut Uncle Tom with ____
23. 'My mother's suffering grew into a ____ in my mind....'

Down
1. White men ____ Uncle Hoskins
2. Helped Richard get library books
3. Set up fight between Richard and Harrison
4. Richard took part in a scheme that skimmed ____ from ticket sales
5. Richard's classmate who gives him advice
6. Elevator operator
7. Richard sold 'anti-Negro' ____
9. Brother Manse's work
10. Advice Griggs gave Richard
13. Shorty operated one
14. Takes Richard to live in Greenwood
15. Richard and Harrison agreed to ____ to fight
17. Aunt Addie was Granny's ____
18. Richard threatened him with razors
21. Landlady in Memphis

Black Boy Crossword 4 Answer Key

							1 S	I	2 N	F	U	L	
				3 O		H			F				4 M
	5 G		6 S	A	L	O	O	N		A			O
7 N	O	R	T	H	I		T		8 K	I	9 T	10 T	E	N
E		I		O	N					N		H		E
W		G		R			11 B	E	S	S		I		Y
S		G		12 T	O	13 W	E	L			U		N	
P		S		Y		L		14 C			R		K	
A			15 P		16 E	L	L	A			A		17 A	
P		18 T		R		V		A		19 A	N	G	E	L
E		20 H	E	L	E	N	A		R			C		L
R		O			T		T		K			E		Y
S		M			E		O		21 M					
		A			N		22 R	A	Z	O	R	S		
		S			D				O					
							23 S	Y	M	B	O	L		

Across
1. Granny thought story books were ____
6. Place where Richard passed time at age 6
7. 'It symbolized to me all I had not felt and seen....'
8. Richard hanged it to get back at his father
11. Willing to marry Richard
12. Granny hit Richard with one when he told her to 'kiss back there'
16. Richard's mother
19. If Richard had seen an ____ like Jacob had, he would have believed, too
20. Wrights had to move from West ____
22. Richard threatened to cut Uncle Tom with ____
23. 'My mother's suffering grew into a ____ in my mind....'

Down
1. White men ____ Uncle Hoskins
2. Helped Richard get library books
3. Set up fight between Richard and Harrison
4. Richard took part in a scheme that skimmed ____ from ticket sales
5. Richard's classmate who gives him advice
6. Elevator operator
7. Richard sold 'anti-Negro' ____
9. Brother Manse's work
10. Advice Griggs gave Richard
13. Shorty operated one
14. Takes Richard to live in Greenwood
15. Richard and Harrison agreed to ____ to fight
17. Aunt Addie was Granny's____
18. Richard threatened him with razors
21. Landlady in Memphis

Black Boy

CRANE	DIED	ELLA	TOWEL	MOSS
CURTAINS	INSURANCE	ELEVATOR	DEATH	REYNOLDS
GREENWOOD	SPEECH	FREE SPACE	RICHARD	HELENA
SHOT	GRIGGS	OLIN	COUNT	VOODOO
HARRISON	SELL	SHORTY	NATHANIEL	ANGEL

Black Boy

THINK	THOMAS	PRETEND	MEMPHIS	JUDGE
KITTEN	NORTH	BESS	ALLY	WRIGHT
MARRY	BAPTIZED	FREE SPACE	ORPHAN	SOLDIERS
FALK	CLARK	GRANDPA	ADDIE	MONEY
GRANNY	SYMBOL	NEWSPAPERS	MAGGIE	AUNT

Black Boy

REYNOLDS	DEATH	CURTAINS	GRANDPA	AUNT
INSURANCE	MAGGIE	KNIFE	DIED	KITTEN
NEWSPAPERS	RAZORS	FREE SPACE	CRANE	COUNT
SELL	MARRY	THOMAS	RICHARD	ELEVATOR
MEMPHIS	MONEY	SALOON	SINFUL	NORTH

Black Boy

FALK	HARRISON	ORPHAN	BESS	SOLDIERS
JUDGE	SYMBOL	ADDIE	GRIGGS	SHOT
GREENWOOD	SIMON	FREE SPACE	VOODOO	ELLA
TOWEL	CLARK	WRIGHT	SPEECH	THINK
OLIN	NATHANIEL	PRETEND	HELENA	MENCKEN

Black Boy

MARRY	VOODOO	SOLDIERS	DIED	OLIN
RICHARD	ALLY	NATHANIEL	MOSS	ELEVATOR
ADDIE	KNIFE	FREE SPACE	NEWSPAPERS	GRANNY
INSURANCE	MENCKEN	GREENWOOD	WRIGHT	FALK
ANGEL	GRANDPA	SELL	RAZORS	ORPHAN

Black Boy

CURTAINS	DEATH	GRIGGS	MONEY	SIMON
TOWEL	JUDGE	BAPTIZED	COUNT	SALOON
MAGGIE	SHORTY	FREE SPACE	BESS	MEMPHIS
HELENA	NORTH	AUNT	HARRISON	SHOT
REYNOLDS	KITTEN	PRETEND	CLARK	ELLA

Black Boy

FALK	KNIFE	TOWEL	THOMAS	MOSS
NATHANIEL	BESS	SIMON	MENCKEN	ELEVATOR
GRANNY	SALOON	FREE SPACE	ANGEL	SOLDIERS
SYMBOL	RAZORS	REYNOLDS	CURTAINS	ALLY
NORTH	HELENA	COUNT	GREENWOOD	SELL

Black Boy

OLIN	DIED	GRIGGS	SHORTY	MARRY
JUDGE	KITTEN	BAPTIZED	PRETEND	MAGGIE
WRIGHT	ADDIE	FREE SPACE	DEATH	THINK
SHOT	VOODOO	MEMPHIS	RICHARD	ORPHAN
HARRISON	CRANE	ELLA	NEWSPAPERS	CLARK

Black Boy

THOMAS	SYMBOL	MEMPHIS	THINK	KNIFE
HARRISON	MOSS	KITTEN	NEWSPAPERS	SOLDIERS
SHORTY	SALOON	FREE SPACE	CRANE	BESS
SIMON	MARRY	OLIN	RICHARD	MAGGIE
GREENWOOD	ORPHAN	WRIGHT	DIED	CURTAINS

Black Boy

SPEECH	HELENA	RAZORS	MENCKEN	MONEY
ADDIE	ALLY	ELLA	PRETEND	CLARK
SINFUL	TOWEL	FREE SPACE	GRIGGS	NORTH
ELEVATOR	DEATH	BAPTIZED	ANGEL	FALK
JUDGE	NATHANIEL	GRANDPA	INSURANCE	VOODOO

Black Boy

HARRISON	NORTH	SIMON	CRANE	SPEECH
FALK	SALOON	WRIGHT	COUNT	REYNOLDS
SHOT	KITTEN	FREE SPACE	SHORTY	MONEY
CLARK	VOODOO	NATHANIEL	THINK	INSURANCE
RAZORS	GRIGGS	MARRY	NEWSPAPERS	PRETEND

Black Boy

MENCKEN	TOWEL	SOLDIERS	SELL	MAGGIE
BAPTIZED	GREENWOOD	RICHARD	ELEVATOR	ALLY
KNIFE	MEMPHIS	FREE SPACE	OLIN	GRANDPA
BESS	SINFUL	AUNT	ORPHAN	ELLA
ANGEL	SYMBOL	MOSS	DIED	JUDGE

Black Boy

RICHARD	COUNT	DEATH	GREENWOOD	ANGEL
SOLDIERS	CRANE	THINK	GRANDPA	MEMPHIS
KITTEN	JUDGE	FREE SPACE	SALOON	ELLA
OLIN	SHOT	FALK	MONEY	SELL
RAZORS	DIED	ORPHAN	ELEVATOR	CLARK

Black Boy

CURTAINS	INSURANCE	TOWEL	REYNOLDS	NEWSPAPERS
AUNT	MAGGIE	SHORTY	GRANNY	SPEECH
WRIGHT	ALLY	FREE SPACE	GRIGGS	SIMON
SYMBOL	KNIFE	NORTH	HARRISON	BESS
THOMAS	MOSS	NATHANIEL	BAPTIZED	MARRY

Black Boy

CURTAINS	GRIGGS	WRIGHT	KITTEN	RAZORS
BAPTIZED	MEMPHIS	JUDGE	THINK	MONEY
HELENA	ADDIE	FREE SPACE	NATHANIEL	ALLY
MOSS	SPEECH	CRANE	SELL	OLIN
NEWSPAPERS	SHOT	DEATH	SYMBOL	REYNOLDS

Black Boy

TOWEL	ORPHAN	VOODOO	NORTH	RICHARD
INSURANCE	ELEVATOR	GRANNY	SOLDIERS	HARRISON
ELLA	ANGEL	FREE SPACE	SIMON	FALK
MENCKEN	SINFUL	SALOON	CLARK	AUNT
THOMAS	MARRY	GREENWOOD	SHORTY	GRANDPA

Black Boy

BESS	THINK	CLARK	HARRISON	SYMBOL
GREENWOOD	HELENA	MOSS	PRETEND	ELEVATOR
DIED	TOWEL	FREE SPACE	SINFUL	RAZORS
SALOON	DEATH	THOMAS	FALK	COUNT
NORTH	GRANNY	INSURANCE	MAGGIE	REYNOLDS

Black Boy

ORPHAN	ELLA	OLIN	SHOT	MARRY
MEMPHIS	SIMON	MONEY	SELL	NEWSPAPERS
BAPTIZED	SPEECH	FREE SPACE	JUDGE	KNIFE
SHORTY	ALLY	CRANE	AUNT	ANGEL
GRANDPA	CURTAINS	WRIGHT	KITTEN	ADDIE

Black Boy

MOSS	SYMBOL	CURTAINS	NEWSPAPERS	GRANDPA
GRIGGS	BESS	REYNOLDS	ANGEL	TOWEL
NATHANIEL	ELLA	FREE SPACE	JUDGE	MENCKEN
DIED	ADDIE	RICHARD	WRIGHT	SALOON
SHOT	THINK	ELEVATOR	GRANNY	NORTH

Black Boy

ALLY	SIMON	MEMPHIS	MAGGIE	INSURANCE
RAZORS	HARRISON	COUNT	GREENWOOD	CRANE
MONEY	SELL	FREE SPACE	MARRY	OLIN
THOMAS	KITTEN	HELENA	ORPHAN	SOLDIERS
PRETEND	AUNT	SINFUL	KNIFE	SPEECH

Black Boy

SHOT	NATHANIEL	THINK	DIED	KITTEN
THOMAS	MOSS	HARRISON	REYNOLDS	JUDGE
TOWEL	GRANNY	FREE SPACE	SINFUL	CRANE
GREENWOOD	GRANDPA	BAPTIZED	BESS	KNIFE
HELENA	ELEVATOR	RAZORS	ANGEL	FALK

Black Boy

MARRY	NORTH	VOODOO	SOLDIERS	SHORTY
DEATH	INSURANCE	SPEECH	WRIGHT	GRIGGS
MONEY	NEWSPAPERS	FREE SPACE	PRETEND	OLIN
AUNT	CURTAINS	ORPHAN	SIMON	MEMPHIS
RICHARD	ADDIE	SELL	SYMBOL	ELLA

Black Boy

INSURANCE	GRANNY	SHOT	ELEVATOR	ALLY
DEATH	MOSS	THINK	PRETEND	NEWSPAPERS
SALOON	COUNT	FREE SPACE	ELLA	CURTAINS
FALK	JUDGE	REYNOLDS	MAGGIE	KNIFE
SIMON	ORPHAN	CRANE	TOWEL	MARRY

Black Boy

GRANDPA	MEMPHIS	GREENWOOD	SOLDIERS	MENCKEN
THOMAS	DIED	RICHARD	VOODOO	ANGEL
NORTH	WRIGHT	FREE SPACE	OLIN	GRIGGS
MONEY	RAZORS	SINFUL	HARRISON	BAPTIZED
NATHANIEL	HELENA	AUNT	SPEECH	SYMBOL

Black Boy

GRANDPA	BESS	AUNT	INSURANCE	TOWEL
SYMBOL	SINFUL	NATHANIEL	GRANNY	ANGEL
MARRY	MONEY	FREE SPACE	PRETEND	ALLY
ORPHAN	VOODOO	NEWSPAPERS	CURTAINS	MAGGIE
HARRISON	SELL	SHOT	HELENA	SPEECH

Black Boy

FALK	DIED	MEMPHIS	NORTH	ELEVATOR
BAPTIZED	WRIGHT	KITTEN	CRANE	ELLA
JUDGE	GREENWOOD	FREE SPACE	MENCKEN	KNIFE
SHORTY	COUNT	CLARK	REYNOLDS	OLIN
THOMAS	RAZORS	ADDIE	RICHARD	SALOON

Black Boy

NATHANIEL	JUDGE	FALK	DEATH	WRIGHT
SIMON	PRETEND	MARRY	MENCKEN	RAZORS
HARRISON	ORPHAN	FREE SPACE	SELL	OLIN
GRIGGS	TOWEL	AUNT	NORTH	MAGGIE
BAPTIZED	MONEY	GRANNY	ELEVATOR	NEWSPAPERS

Black Boy

RICHARD	ADDIE	SHORTY	VOODOO	ALLY
GRANDPA	SINFUL	MOSS	KITTEN	CURTAINS
THINK	SALOON	FREE SPACE	SYMBOL	DIED
REYNOLDS	GREENWOOD	SOLDIERS	HELENA	CRANE
ANGEL	CLARK	ELLA	THOMAS	COUNT

Black Boy

ANGEL	THINK	REYNOLDS	FALK	SYMBOL
JUDGE	CLARK	GRANNY	AUNT	DIED
RAZORS	DEATH	FREE SPACE	COUNT	GRIGGS
WRIGHT	VOODOO	SALOON	SELL	HARRISON
MONEY	NORTH	SPEECH	SIMON	MARRY

Black Boy

MOSS	SINFUL	CURTAINS	GRANDPA	ALLY
MENCKEN	TOWEL	MAGGIE	THOMAS	OLIN
KNIFE	NEWSPAPERS	FREE SPACE	CRANE	INSURANCE
SHORTY	HELENA	GREENWOOD	SOLDIERS	NATHANIEL
MEMPHIS	ADDIE	KITTEN	BESS	ORPHAN

Black Boy

RICHARD	TOWEL	SINFUL	BAPTIZED	HELENA
INSURANCE	ORPHAN	BESS	JUDGE	GRIGGS
SELL	SHORTY	FREE SPACE	SALOON	SPEECH
REYNOLDS	KNIFE	SIMON	ELEVATOR	SHOT
OLIN	ELLA	SOLDIERS	MEMPHIS	CURTAINS

Black Boy

DEATH	KITTEN	ALLY	AUNT	MENCKEN
FALK	SYMBOL	GREENWOOD	MONEY	CRANE
GRANDPA	THOMAS	FREE SPACE	DIED	MAGGIE
THINK	CLARK	NEWSPAPERS	VOODOO	NORTH
RAZORS	ANGEL	HARRISON	NATHANIEL	ADDIE

Black Boy Vocabulary Word List

No.	Word	Clue/Definition
1.	ACUTE	Sharp or severe; intense
2.	ANTAGONISM	Hostility that results in active resistance or oppression
3.	ANXIETY	A state of uneasiness and apprehension
4.	ARDENTLY	Characterized by strong enthusiasm or devotion
5.	ASPIRATIONS	Ambitions
6.	AURA	Atmosphere
7.	AVAILED	Made use of
8.	BAFFLED	Puzzled; confused
9.	BANTERING	Speaking in a playful or teasing way
10.	BLASPHEMY	To speak of God in an irreverent manner
11.	BOON	A benefit
12.	CAPITULATE	Surrender; give up
13.	CONSPICUOUSLY	Obviously
14.	CONTEMPLATE	Thing about
15.	CONTEMPTUOUS	Scornful
16.	CRYPTIC	Tending to conceal or camouflage
17.	DEBASED	Lowered in character, quality or value
18.	DELUSION	A false belief or opinion
19.	DENUNCIATION	Public condemnation or censure
20.	DEVASTATED	Destroyed
21.	DEVOID	Completely lacking or empty
22.	DISSEMBLE	To disguise one's real nature, motives or feelings
23.	DOUR	Silently ill-humored or sternly obstinate
24.	DUBIOUS	Doubtful
25.	EMULATE	Imitate
26.	ENTHRALLED	Spellbound; captivated
27.	EXPLOITED	Made use of selfishly or unethically
28.	FEIGNED	Gave a false appearance of; pretended
29.	FIAT	An order or authorization
30.	FRENZY	A state of violent or wild excitement
31.	HYPOTHETICAL	Suppositional
32.	IMPETUS	An impelling force
33.	IMPLACABLE	Impossible to please or satisfy
34.	IMPLORING	Making an earnest appeal
35.	IMPUDENT	Offensively bold
36.	INCONCEIVABLE	Impossible to comprehend or fully grasp
37.	INCRIMINATING	Causing to appear guilty of a crime or fault
38.	INCURRED	Acquired
39.	INDUCED	Caused
40.	INDULGENTLY	Leniently; patiently
41.	INTRIGUE	A secret or underhanded scheme
42.	INTUITIVELY	Without the use of rational reasoning; instinctively
43.	INVECTIVES	Abusive language
44.	LARCENOUS	Characterized by theft
45.	LIEU	In place of
46.	LIVID	Discolored; showing extreme anger
47.	LOITERING	Standing idly about; lingering with no purpose
48.	MOROSE	Gloomy
49.	NONCHALANTLY	Seeming to be coolly unconcerned or indifferent
50.	NOSTALGIA	A bittersweet longing for things of the past
51.	NUANCE	Subtle or slight degree of difference

Black Boy Vocabulary Word List

No.	Word	Clue/Definition
52.	OBSTINACY	Stubbornness
53.	OVERTONE	An ulterior meaning or quality; an implication or hint
54.	PATRONIZING	Going to as a customer
55.	PEERING	Looking intently or searchingly
56.	PETTY	Trivial
57.	PLIABLE	Easily influenced or persuaded
58.	PREDILECTION	Preference
59.	PRESUME	Take for granted as being true
60.	PROVOCATIONS	Something that incites or is intended to cause trouble
61.	QUALMS	Uneasy feelings about the rightness of an action
62.	RECONDITE	Not easily understood
63.	RELENTLESSLY	Steadily; persistently
64.	REPUGNANT	Offensive or repulsive
65.	REVEL	To take great pleasure or delight
66.	RITUAL	Ceremony
67.	ROUSED	Excited as to anger or action; stirred up
68.	SAUCILY	Disrespectfully
69.	SAUNTERED	Strolled
70.	SOLICITUDE	Care or concern for the well-being of another
71.	SOLIDARITY	A union of interests or purposes among group members
72.	SQUALOR	A filthy and wretched condition
73.	SUBSERVIENCE	Being subordinate; of a lesser position
74.	SURREPTITIOUSLY	Stealthily
75.	TANTAMOUNT	Equivalent in effect or value
76.	TAUT	Tight; tense
77.	VINDICTIVE	Revengeful
78.	VIVID	Heard, seen or felt as if real
79.	WANED	Approached an end
80.	WAYLAYING	Ambushing; intercepting someone unexpectedly
81.	YEARNED	Had a strong, often melancholy desire

Black Boy Vocabulary Fill In The Blank 1

_____ 1. Not easily understood

_____ 2. Leniently; patiently

_____ 3. Easily influenced or persuaded

_____ 4. Causing to appear guilty of a crime or fault

_____ 5. Scornful

_____ 6. A union of interests or purposes among group members

_____ 7. An ulterior meaning or quality; an implication or hint

_____ 8. Surrender; give up

_____ 9. Puzzled; confused

_____ 10. Obviously

_____ 11. Lowered in character, quality or value

_____ 12. Hostility that results in active resistance or oppression

_____ 13. Discolored; showing extreme anger

_____ 14. Impossible to comprehend or fully grasp

_____ 15. Speaking in a playful or teasing way

_____ 16. Offensive or repulsive

_____ 17. Public condemnation or censure

_____ 18. A state of violent or wild excitement

_____ 19. Impossible to please or satisfy

_____ 20. Without the use of rational reasoning; instinctively

Black Boy Vocabulary Fill In The Blank 1 Answer Key

RECONDITE	1. Not easily understood
INDULGENTLY	2. Leniently; patiently
PLIABLE	3. Easily influenced or persuaded
INCRIMINATING	4. Causing to appear guilty of a crime or fault
CONTEMPTUOUS	5. Scornful
SOLIDARITY	6. A union of interests or purposes among group members
OVERTONE	7. An ulterior meaning or quality; an implication or hint
CAPITULATE	8. Surrender; give up
BAFFLED	9. Puzzled; confused
CONSPICUOUSLY	10. Obviously
DEBASED	11. Lowered in character, quality or value
ANTAGONISM	12. Hostility that results in active resistance or oppression
LIVID	13. Discolored; showing extreme anger
INCONCEIVABLE	14. Impossible to comprehend or fully grasp
BANTERING	15. Speaking in a playful or teasing way
REPUGNANT	16. Offensive or repulsive
DENUNCIATION	17. Public condemnation or censure
FRENZY	18. A state of violent or wild excitement
IMPLACABLE	19. Impossible to please or satisfy
INTUITIVELY	20. Without the use of rational reasoning; instinctively

Copyrighted

Black Boy Vocabulary Fill In The Blank 2

_____ 1. Made use of

_____ 2. Scornful

_____ 3. Atmosphere

_____ 4. A false belief or opinion

_____ 5. An order or authorization

_____ 6. A union of interests or purposes among group members

_____ 7. Strolled

_____ 8. Made use of selfishly or unethically

_____ 9. Heard, seen or felt as if real

_____ 10. A secret or underhanded scheme

_____ 11. Disrespectfully

_____ 12. Standing idly about; lingering with no purpose

_____ 13. Imitate

_____ 14. A bittersweet longing for things of the past

_____ 15. Stealthily

_____ 16. Had a strong, often melancholy desire

_____ 17. Seeming to be coolly unconcerned or indifferent

_____ 18. Care or concern for the well-being of another

_____ 19. A state of violent or wild excitement

_____ 20. Without the use of rational reasoning; instinctively

Black Boy Vocabulary Fill In The Blank 2 Answer Key

AVAILED	1. Made use of
CONTEMPTUOUS	2. Scornful
AURA	3. Atmosphere
DELUSION	4. A false belief or opinion
FIAT	5. An order or authorization
SOLIDARITY	6. A union of interests or purposes among group members
SAUNTERED	7. Strolled
EXPLOITED	8. Made use of selfishly or unethically
VIVID	9. Heard, seen or felt as if real
INTRIGUE	10. A secret or underhanded scheme
SAUCILY	11. Disrespectfully
LOITERING	12. Standing idly about; lingering with no purpose
EMULATE	13. Imitate
NOSTALGIA	14. A bittersweet longing for things of the past
SURREPTITIOUSLY	15. Stealthily
YEARNED	16. Had a strong, often melancholy desire
NONCHALANTLY	17. Seeming to be coolly unconcerned or indifferent
SOLICITUDE	18. Care or concern for the well-being of another
FRENZY	19. A state of violent or wild excitement
INTUITIVELY	20. Without the use of rational reasoning; instinctively

Black Boy Vocabulary Fill In The Blank 3

_____ 1. Excited as to anger or action; stirred up

_____ 2. Stubbornness

_____ 3. Thing about

_____ 4. To take great pleasure or delight

_____ 5. Abusive language

_____ 6. Being subordinate; of a lesser position

_____ 7. Impossible to please or satisfy

_____ 8. Steadily; persistently

_____ 9. Made use of

_____ 10. Made use of selfishly or unethically

_____ 11. Strolled

_____ 12. A secret or underhanded scheme

_____ 13. Characterized by strong enthusiasm or devotion

_____ 14. Not easily understood

_____ 15. Suppositional

_____ 16. Disrespectfully

_____ 17. Had a strong, often melancholy desire

_____ 18. Causing to appear guilty of a crime or fault

_____ 19. Standing idly about; lingering with no purpose

_____ 20. Ambushing; intercepting someone unexpectedly

Black Boy Vocabulary Fill In The Blank 3 Answer Key

ROUSED	1. Excited as to anger or action; stirred up
OBSTINACY	2. Stubbornness
CONTEMPLATE	3. Thing about
REVEL	4. To take great pleasure or delight
INVECTIVES	5. Abusive language
SUBSERVIENCE	6. Being subordinate; of a lesser position
IMPLACABLE	7. Impossible to please or satisfy
RELENTLESSLY	8. Steadily; persistently
AVAILED	9. Made use of
EXPLOITED	10. Made use of selfishly or unethically
SAUNTERED	11. Strolled
INTRIGUE	12. A secret or underhanded scheme
ARDENTLY	13. Characterized by strong enthusiasm or devotion
RECONDITE	14. Not easily understood
HYPOTHETICAL	15. Suppositional
SAUCILY	16. Disrespectfully
YEARNED	17. Had a strong, often melancholy desire
INCRIMINATING	18. Causing to appear guilty of a crime or fault
LOITERING	19. Standing idly about; lingering with no purpose
WAYLAYING	20. Ambushing; intercepting someone unexpectedly

Black Boy Vocabulary Fill In The Blank 4

_____

1. Stealthily
2. Atmosphere
3. Being subordinate; of a lesser position
4. Thing about
5. Speaking in a playful or teasing way
6. Made use of selfishly or unethically
7. Uneasy feelings about the rightness of an action
8. Equivalent in effect or value
9. Heard, seen or felt as if real
10. Standing idly about; lingering with no purpose
11. Public condemnation or censure
12. A benefit
13. Surrender; give up
14. Subtle or slight degree of difference
15. An ulterior meaning or quality; an implication or hint
16. Silently ill-humored or sternly obstinate
17. Spellbound; captivated
18. Caused
19. To disguise one's real nature, motives or feelings
20. Completely lacking or empty

Black Boy Vocabulary Fill In The Blank 4 Answer Key

SURREPTITIOUSLY	1. Stealthily
AURA	2. Atmosphere
SUBSERVIENCE	3. Being subordinate; of a lesser position
CONTEMPLATE	4. Thing about
BANTERING	5. Speaking in a playful or teasing way
EXPLOITED	6. Made use of selfishly or unethically
QUALMS	7. Uneasy feelings about the rightness of an action
TANTAMOUNT	8. Equivalent in effect or value
VIVID	9. Heard, seen or felt as if real
LOITERING	10. Standing idly about; lingering with no purpose
DENUNCIATION	11. Public condemnation or censure
BOON	12. A benefit
CAPITULATE	13. Surrender; give up
NUANCE	14. Subtle or slight degree of difference
OVERTONE	15. An ulterior meaning or quality; an implication or hint
DOUR	16. Silently ill-humored or sternly obstinate
ENTHRALLED	17. Spellbound; captivated
INDUCED	18. Caused
DISSEMBLE	19. To disguise one's real nature, motives or feelings
DEVOID	20. Completely lacking or empty

Black Boy Vocabulary Matching 1

___ 1. PEERING
___ 2. PLIABLE
___ 3. RECONDITE
___ 4. INTRIGUE
___ 5. IMPETUS
___ 6. INVECTIVES
___ 7. CONSPICUOUSLY
___ 8. IMPUDENT
___ 9. INDUCED
___ 10. IMPLACABLE
___ 11. SAUCILY
___ 12. FRENZY
___ 13. SURREPTITIOUSLY
___ 14. NUANCE
___ 15. IMPLORING
___ 16. REVEL
___ 17. CAPITULATE
___ 18. PETTY
___ 19. INTUITIVELY
___ 20. TAUT
___ 21. DENUNCIATION
___ 22. BLASPHEMY
___ 23. DISSEMBLE
___ 24. INCURRED
___ 25. SQUALOR

A. Easily influenced or persuaded
B. A secret or underhanded scheme
C. Subtle or slight degree of difference
D. An impelling force
E. Not easily understood
F. Looking intently or searchingly
G. Offensively bold
H. To take great pleasure or delight
I. Abusive language
J. Without the use of rational reasoning; instinctively
K. Disrespectfully
L. Stealthily
M. Obviously
N. To speak of God in an irreverent manner
O. Caused
P. Trivial
Q. Making an earnest appeal
R. A filthy and wretched condition
S. Acquired
T. Impossible to please or satisfy
U. A state of violent or wild excitement
V. Public condemnation or censure
W. Tight; tense
X. Surrender; give up
Y. To disguise one's real nature, motives or feelings

Black Boy Vocabulary Matching 1 Answer Key

F - 1. PEERING		A. Easily influenced or persuaded
A - 2. PLIABLE		B. A secret or underhanded scheme
E - 3. RECONDITE		C. Subtle or slight degree of difference
B - 4. INTRIGUE		D. An impelling force
D - 5. IMPETUS		E. Not easily understood
I - 6. INVECTIVES		F. Looking intently or searchingly
M - 7. CONSPICUOUSLY		G. Offensively bold
G - 8. IMPUDENT		H. To take great pleasure or delight
O - 9. INDUCED		I. Abusive language
T - 10. IMPLACABLE		J. Without the use of rational reasoning; instinctively
K - 11. SAUCILY		K. Disrespectfully
U - 12. FRENZY		L. Stealthily
L - 13. SURREPTITIOUSLY		M. Obviously
C - 14. NUANCE		N. To speak of God in an irreverent manner
Q - 15. IMPLORING		O. Caused
H - 16. REVEL		P. Trivial
X - 17. CAPITULATE		Q. Making an earnest appeal
P - 18. PETTY		R. A filthy and wretched condition
J - 19. INTUITIVELY		S. Acquired
W - 20. TAUT		T. Impossible to please or satisfy
V - 21. DENUNCIATION		U. A state of violent or wild excitement
N - 22. BLASPHEMY		V. Public condemnation or censure
Y - 23. DISSEMBLE		W. Tight; tense
S - 24. INCURRED		X. Surrender; give up
R - 25. SQUALOR		Y. To disguise one's real nature, motives or feelings

Black Boy Vocabulary Matching 2

___ 1. LIEU
___ 2. INCRIMINATING
___ 3. IMPUDENT
___ 4. BOON
___ 5. CONSPICUOUSLY
___ 6. SAUCILY
___ 7. ANXIETY
___ 8. ENTHRALLED
___ 9. PLIABLE
___10. FIAT
___11. INTUITIVELY
___12. AURA
___13. INVECTIVES
___14. PEERING
___15. INCURRED
___16. ASPIRATIONS
___17. PRESUME
___18. IMPLACABLE
___19. INDUCED
___20. OBSTINACY
___21. LOITERING
___22. INTRIGUE
___23. INCONCEIVABLE
___24. IMPLORING
___25. ACUTE

A. Take for granted as being true
B. Stubbornness
C. Easily influenced or persuaded
D. Obviously
E. Looking intently or searchingly
F. Sharp or severe; intense
G. A secret or underhanded scheme
H. Spellbound; captivated
I. A state of uneasiness and apprehension
J. Without the use of rational reasoning; instinctively
K. In place of
L. Disrespectfully
M. Causing to appear guilty of a crime or fault
N. Ambitions
O. Atmosphere
P. Acquired
Q. Standing idly about; lingering with no purpose
R. Making an earnest appeal
S. Impossible to comprehend or fully grasp
T. Offensively bold
U. Abusive language
V. Impossible to please or satisfy
W. A benefit
X. An order or authorization
Y. Caused

Black Boy Vocabulary Matching 2 Answer Key

K - 1. LIEU	A.	Take for granted as being true
M - 2. INCRIMINATING	B.	Stubbornness
T - 3. IMPUDENT	C.	Easily influenced or persuaded
W - 4. BOON	D.	Obviously
D - 5. CONSPICUOUSLY	E.	Looking intently or searchingly
L - 6. SAUCILY	F.	Sharp or severe; intense
I - 7. ANXIETY	G.	A secret or underhanded scheme
H - 8. ENTHRALLED	H.	Spellbound; captivated
C - 9. PLIABLE	I.	A state of uneasiness and apprehension
X - 10. FIAT	J.	Without the use of rational reasoning; instinctively
J - 11. INTUITIVELY	K.	In place of
O - 12. AURA	L.	Disrespectfully
U - 13. INVECTIVES	M.	Causing to appear guilty of a crime or fault
E - 14. PEERING	N.	Ambitions
P - 15. INCURRED	O.	Atmosphere
N - 16. ASPIRATIONS	P.	Acquired
A - 17. PRESUME	Q.	Standing idly about; lingering with no purpose
V - 18. IMPLACABLE	R.	Making an earnest appeal
Y - 19. INDUCED	S.	Impossible to comprehend or fully grasp
B - 20. OBSTINACY	T.	Offensively bold
Q - 21. LOITERING	U.	Abusive language
G - 22. INTRIGUE	V.	Impossible to please or satisfy
S - 23. INCONCEIVABLE	W.	A benefit
R - 24. IMPLORING	X.	An order or authorization
F - 25. ACUTE	Y.	Caused

Black Boy Vocabulary Matching 3

___ 1. PREDILECTION   A. Going to as a customer
___ 2. PEERING   B. Offensive or repulsive
___ 3. REPUGNANT   C. Not easily understood
___ 4. ACUTE   D. Made use of
___ 5. SAUCILY   E. Thing about
___ 6. LIVID   F. Destroyed
___ 7. WANED   G. Preference
___ 8. INCRIMINATING   H. Abusive language
___ 9. FRENZY   I. Without the use of rational reasoning; instinctively
___10. RITUAL   J. Sharp or severe; intense
___11. AVAILED   K. Approached an end
___12. INVECTIVES   L. Looking intently or searchingly
___13. WAYLAYING   M. Ambushing; intercepting someone unexpectedly
___14. TANTAMOUNT   N. Causing to appear guilty of a crime or fault
___15. INTUITIVELY   O. An impelling force
___16. FEIGNED   P. An order or authorization
___17. CONTEMPLATE   Q. Disrespectfully
___18. IMPETUS   R. A state of violent or wild excitement
___19. PROVOCATIONS   S. Ceremony
___20. PATRONIZING   T. Seeming to be coolly unconcerned or indifferent
___21. DEVASTATED   U. A union of interests or purposes among group members
___22. NONCHALANTLY   V. Equivalent in effect or value
___23. FIAT   W. Discolored; showing extreme anger
___24. SOLIDARITY   X. Gave a false appearance of; pretended
___25. RECONDITE   Y. Something that incites or is intended to cause trouble

Black Boy Vocabulary Matching 3 Answer Key

G - 1. PREDILECTION	A.	Going to as a customer
L - 2. PEERING	B.	Offensive or repulsive
B - 3. REPUGNANT	C.	Not easily understood
J - 4. ACUTE	D.	Made use of
Q - 5. SAUCILY	E.	Thing about
W - 6. LIVID	F.	Destroyed
K - 7. WANED	G.	Preference
N - 8. INCRIMINATING	H.	Abusive language
R - 9. FRENZY	I.	Without the use of rational reasoning; instinctively
S - 10. RITUAL	J.	Sharp or severe; intense
D - 11. AVAILED	K.	Approached an end
H - 12. INVECTIVES	L.	Looking intently or searchingly
M - 13. WAYLAYING	M.	Ambushing; intercepting someone unexpectedly
V - 14. TANTAMOUNT	N.	Causing to appear guilty of a crime or fault
I - 15. INTUITIVELY	O.	An impelling force
X - 16. FEIGNED	P.	An order or authorization
E - 17. CONTEMPLATE	Q.	Disrespectfully
O - 18. IMPETUS	R.	A state of violent or wild excitement
Y - 19. PROVOCATIONS	S.	Ceremony
A - 20. PATRONIZING	T.	Seeming to be coolly unconcerned or indifferent
F - 21. DEVASTATED	U.	A union of interests or purposes among group members
T - 22. NONCHALANTLY	V.	Equivalent in effect or value
P - 23. FIAT	W.	Discolored; showing extreme anger
U - 24. SOLIDARITY	X.	Gave a false appearance of; pretended
C - 25. RECONDITE	Y.	Something that incites or is intended to cause trouble

Black Boy Vocabulary Matching 4 Answer Key

___ 1. DELUSION   A. Going to as a customer
___ 2. DOUR   B. Made use of selfishly or unethically
___ 3. ACUTE   C. Imitate
___ 4. SUBSERVIENCE   D. Atmosphere
___ 5. OBSTINACY   E. A secret or underhanded scheme
___ 6. SURREPTITIOUSLY   F. Strolled
___ 7. OVERTONE   G. Hostility that results in active resistance or oppression
___ 8. IMPLACABLE   H. Lowered in character, quality or value
___ 9. ANTAGONISM   I. Surrender; give up
___10. RECONDITE   J. A false belief or opinion
___11. INTRIGUE   K. A filthy and wretched condition
___12. EMULATE   L. Impossible to please or satisfy
___13. REVEL   M. Being subordinate; of a lesser position
___14. DUBIOUS   N. An ulterior meaning or quality; an implication or hint
___15. RITUAL   O. Doubtful
___16. EXPLOITED   P. Stubbornness
___17. PATRONIZING   Q. Silently ill-humored or sternly obstinate
___18. AURA   R. Not easily understood
___19. SQUALOR   S. Stealthily
___20. CONSPICUOUSLY   T. Obviously
___21. DEBASED   U. Ceremony
___22. LIEU   V. Sharp or severe; intense
___23. NUANCE   W. Subtle or slight degree of difference
___24. SAUNTERED   X. To take great pleasure or delight
___25. CAPITULATE   Y. In place of

Black Boy Vocabulary Matching 4 Answer Key

J - 1. DELUSION	A. Going to as a customer
Q - 2. DOUR	B. Made use of selfishly or unethically
V - 3. ACUTE	C. Imitate
M - 4. SUBSERVIENCE	D. Atmosphere
P - 5. OBSTINACY	E. A secret or underhanded scheme
S - 6. SURREPTITIOUSLY	F. Strolled
N - 7. OVERTONE	G. Hostility that results in active resistance or oppression
L - 8. IMPLACABLE	H. Lowered in character, quality or value
G - 9. ANTAGONISM	I. Surrender; give up
R - 10. RECONDITE	J. A false belief or opinion
E - 11. INTRIGUE	K. A filthy and wretched condition
C - 12. EMULATE	L. Impossible to please or satisfy
X - 13. REVEL	M. Being subordinate; of a lesser position
O - 14. DUBIOUS	N. An ulterior meaning or quality; an implication or hint
U - 15. RITUAL	O. Doubtful
B - 16. EXPLOITED	P. Stubbornness
A - 17. PATRONIZING	Q. Silently ill-humored or sternly obstinate
D - 18. AURA	R. Not easily understood
K - 19. SQUALOR	S. Stealthily
T - 20. CONSPICUOUSLY	T. Obviously
H - 21. DEBASED	U. Ceremony
Y - 22. LIEU	V. Sharp or severe; intense
W - 23. NUANCE	W. Subtle or slight degree of difference
F - 24. SAUNTERED	X. To take great pleasure or delight
I - 25. CAPITULATE	Y. In place of

Black Boy Vocabulary Magic Squares 1

Match the definition with the vocabulary word. Put your answers in the magic squares below. When your answers are correct, all columns and rows will add to the same number.

A. LIEU
B. SOLIDARITY
C. AURA
D. EXPLOITED
E. ROUSED
F. CONTEMPLATE
G. VIVID
H. DISSEMBLE
I. IMPLACABLE
J. RELENTLESSLY
K. OBSTINACY
L. TAUT
M. DEVOID
N. PRESUME
O. REVEL
P. CONTEMPTUOUS

1. To disguise one's real nature, motives or feelings
2. Completely lacking or empty
3. A union of interests or purposes among group members
4. Stubbornness
5. Steadily; persistently
6. Atmosphere
7. Scornful
8. Excited as to anger or action; stirred up
9. To take great pleasure or delight
10. Thing about
11. Impossible to please or satisfy
12. Made use of selfishly or unethically
13. In place of
14. Tight; tense
15. Heard, seen or felt as if real
16. Take for granted as being true

A=	B=	C=	D=
E=	F=	G=	H=
I=	J=	K=	L=
M=	N=	O=	P=

Black Boy Vocabulary Magic Sqaures 1 Answer Key

Match the definition with the vocabulary word. Put your answers in the magic squares below. When your answers are correct, all columns and rows will add to the same number.

A. LIEU
B. SOLIDARITY
C. AURA
D. EXPLOITED
E. ROUSED
F. CONTEMPLATE
G. VIVID
H. DISSEMBLE
I. IMPLACABLE
J. RELENTLESSLY
K. OBSTINACY
L. TAUT
M. DEVOID
N. PRESUME
O. REVEL
P. CONTEMPTUOUS

1. To disguise one's real nature, motives or feelings
2. Completely lacking or empty
3. A union of interests or purposes among group members
4. Stubbornness
5. Steadily; persistently
6. Atmosphere
7. Scornful
8. Excited as to anger or action; stirred up
9. To take great pleasure or delight
10. Thing about
11. Impossible to please or satisfy
12. Made use of selfishly or unethically
13. In place of
14. Tight; tense
15. Heard, seen or felt as if real
16. Take for granted as being true

A=13	B=3	C=6	D=12
E=8	F=10	G=15	H=1
I=11	J=5	K=4	L=14
M=2	N=16	O=9	P=7

Black Boy Vocabulary Magic Squares 2

Match the definition with the vocabulary word. Put your answers in the magic squares below. When your answers are correct, all columns and rows will add to the same number.

A. INDUCED
B. DENUNCIATION
C. PATRONIZING
D. IMPLACABLE
E. SAUNTERED
F. MOROSE
G. ASPIRATIONS
H. DOUR
I. INCURRED
J. REPUGNANT
K. OVERTONE
L. EXPLOITED
M. CONTEMPLATE
N. PROVOCATIONS
O. DELUSION
P. NUANCE

1. A false belief or opinion
2. Offensive or repulsive
3. Silently ill-humored or sternly obstinate
4. Caused
5. Impossible to please or satisfy
6. Strolled
7. An ulterior meaning or quality; an implication or hint
8. Something that incites or is intended to cause trouble
9. Gloomy
10. Going to as a customer
11. Thing about
12. Made use of selfishly or unethically
13. Acquired
14. Subtle or slight degree of difference
15. Public condemnation or censure
16. Ambitions

A=	B=	C=	D=
E=	F=	G=	H=
I=	J=	K=	L=
M=	N=	O=	P=

Black Boy Vocabulary Magic Squares 2 Answer Key

Match the definition with the vocabulary word. Put your answers in the magic squares below. When your answers are correct, all columns and rows will add to the same number.

A. INDUCED
B. DENUNCIATION
C. PATRONIZING
D. IMPLACABLE
E. SAUNTERED
F. MOROSE
G. ASPIRATIONS
H. DOUR
I. INCURRED
J. REPUGNANT
K. OVERTONE
L. EXPLOITED
M. CONTEMPLATE
N. PROVOCATIONS
O. DELUSION
P. NUANCE

1. A false belief or opinion
2. Offensive or repulsive
3. Silently ill-humored or sternly obstinate
4. Caused
5. Impossible to please or satisfy
6. Strolled
7. An ulterior meaning or quality; an implication or hint
8. Something that incites or is intended to cause trouble
9. Gloomy
10. Going to as a customer
11. Thing about
12. Made use of selfishly or unethically
13. Acquired
14. Subtle or slight degree of difference
15. Public condemnation or censure
16. Ambitions

A=4	B=15	C=10	D=5
E=6	F=9	G=16	H=3
I=13	J=2	K=7	L=12
M=11	N=8	O=1	P=14

Black Boy Vocabulary Magic Squares 3

Match the definition with the vocabulary word. Put your answers in the magic squares below. When your answers are correct, all columns and rows will add to the same number.

A. BANTERING
B. DEBASED
C. SOLICITUDE
D. NONCHALANTLY
E. WANED
F. RITUAL
G. FRENZY
H. REPUGNANT
I. DENUNCIATION
J. ROUSED
K. RECONDITE
L. PREDILECTION
M. YEARNED
N. AVAILED
O. IMPUDENT
P. MOROSE

1. Ceremony
2. Public condemnation or censure
3. Offensively bold
4. Seeming to be coolly unconcerned or indifferent
5. Had a strong, often melancholy desire
6. Lowered in character, quality or value
7. Offensive or repulsive
8. Not easily understood
9. Care or concern for the well-being of another
10. Gloomy
11. Excited as to anger or action; stirred up
12. Approached an end
13. Preference
14. A state of violent or wild excitement
15. Speaking in a playful or teasing way
16. Made use of

A=	B=	C=	D=
E=	F=	G=	H=
I=	J=	K=	L=
M=	N=	O=	P=

Black Boy Vocabulary Magic Squares 3 Answer Key

Match the definition with the vocabulary word. Put your answers in the magic squares below. When your answers are correct, all columns and rows will add to the same number.

A. BANTERING
B. DEBASED
C. SOLICITUDE
D. NONCHALANTLY
E. WANED
F. RITUAL
G. FRENZY
H. REPUGNANT
I. DENUNCIATION
J. ROUSED
K. RECONDITE
L. PREDILECTION
M. YEARNED
N. AVAILED
O. IMPUDENT
P. MOROSE

1. Ceremony
2. Public condemnation or censure
3. Offensively bold
4. Seeming to be coolly unconcerned or indifferent
5. Had a strong, often melancholy desire
6. Lowered in character, quality or value
7. Offensive or repulsive
8. Not easily understood
9. Care or concern for the well-being of another
10. Gloomy
11. Excited as to anger or action; stirred up
12. Approached an end
13. Preference
14. A state of violent or wild excitement
15. Speaking in a playful or teasing way
16. Made use of

A=15	B=6	C=9	D=4
E=12	F=1	G=14	H=7
I=2	J=11	K=8	L=13
M=5	N=16	O=3	P=10

Black Boy Vocabulary Magic Squares 4

Match the definition with the vocabulary word. Put your answers in the magic squares below. When your answers are correct, all columns and rows will add to the same number.

A. BAFFLED
B. IMPLACABLE
C. DEVASTATED
D. TANTAMOUNT
E. IMPUDENT
F. CONSPICUOUSLY
G. SAUCILY
H. DUBIOUS
I. INCURRED
J. DEBASED
K. INDULGENTLY
L. ACUTE
M. SQUALOR
N. WAYLAYING
O. OVERTONE
P. ENTHRALLED

1. Impossible to please or satisfy
2. Disrespectfully
3. Leniently; patiently
4. Ambushing; intercepting someone unexpectedly
5. A filthy and wretched condition
6. Sharp or severe; intense
7. Doubtful
8. Puzzled; confused
9. Spellbound; captivated
10. Acquired
11. Offensively bold
12. Equivalent in effect or value
13. Destroyed
14. Obviously
15. Lowered in character, quality or value
16. An ulterior meaning or quality; an implication or hint

A=	B=	C=	D=
E=	F=	G=	H=
I=	J=	K=	L=
M=	N=	O=	P=

Black Boy Vocabulary Magic Squares 4 Answer Key

Match the definition with the vocabulary word. Put your answers in the magic squares below. When your answers are correct, all columns and rows will add to the same number.

A. BAFFLED
B. IMPLACABLE
C. DEVASTATED
D. TANTAMOUNT
E. IMPUDENT
F. CONSPICUOUSLY
G. SAUCILY
H. DUBIOUS
I. INCURRED
J. DEBASED
K. INDULGENTLY
L. ACUTE
M. SQUALOR
N. WAYLAYING
O. OVERTONE
P. ENTHRALLED

1. Impossible to please or satisfy
2. Disrespectfully
3. Leniently; patiently
4. Ambushing; intercepting someone unexpectedly
5. A filthy and wretched condition
6. Sharp or severe; intense
7. Doubtful
8. Puzzled; confused
9. Spellbound; captivated
10. Acquired
11. Offensively bold
12. Equivalent in effect or value
13. Destroyed
14. Obviously
15. Lowered in character, quality or value
16. An ulterior meaning or quality; an implication or hint

A=8	B=1	C=13	D=12
E=11	F=14	G=2	H=7
I=10	J=15	K=3	L=6
M=5	N=4	O=16	P=9

Black Boy Vocabulary Word Search 1

```
A N T A G O N I S M D N S A U C I L Y Q
S N N I P P D O V J I U U B A F F L E D
P F X Z M F D V I L V R B A M O R O S E
I Z I I J P P E V K I X K I N P Y E D M
R O M A E X E R I J L L K Q O C Q T C W
A B P D C T J T D F I E W X F U E A N H
T S U Z H U Y O U N H V L L R M S L W Y
I T D R V Y T N V S K E A P E G F U S N
O I E N O G D E L L A R H T N E P M F R
N N N Y N U C P D M C P E I Z M L E E J
S A T Y P T S L H E T G Y P Y A W K I K
L C P L I D F E N J L A P P U T F D G V
M Y V V I J D O D Y L U I Q E G R M N B
Q L E O D E U O D Y E P S N N T N H E Z
W S V T S S U E A W V A L I T T T A D V
B E A A Y R C W A U R A R I O R W Y N C
D I B Z V U J N B M G E X N A N I W P T
F E F Q D D E J O T E X S H E B W G Z Q
D R S N N D P P O P T A U T M D L V U F
K C I T P Y R C N P R E S U M E Y E G E
```

A benefit (4)
A false belief or opinion (8)
A secret or underhanded scheme (8)
A state of uneasiness and apprehension (7)
A state of violent or wild excitement (6)
Abusive language (10)
Ambitions (11)
Ambushing; intercepting someone unexpectedly (9)
An impelling force (7)
An order or authorization (4)
An ulterior meaning or quality; an implication or hint (8)
Approached an end (5)
Atmosphere (4)
Caused (7)
Characterized by theft (9)
Completely lacking or empty (6)
Discolored; showing extreme anger (5)
Disrespectfully (7)
Doubtful (7)
Easily influenced or persuaded (7)
Excited as to anger or action; stirred up (6)
Gave a false appearance of; pretended (7)

Gloomy (6)
Had a strong, often melancholy desire (7)
Heard, seen or felt as if real (5)
Hostility that results in active resistance or oppression (10)
Imitate (7)
In place of (4)
Looking intently or searchingly (7)
Lowered in character, quality or value (7)
Offensive or repulsive (9)
Offensively bold (8)
Puzzled; confused (7)
Sharp or severe; intense (5)
Silently ill-humored or sternly obstinate (4)
Spellbound; captivated (10)
Stubbornness (9)
Subtle or slight degree of difference (6)
Take for granted as being true (7)
Tending to conceal or camouflage (7)
Tight; tense (4)
To take great pleasure or delight (5)
Trivial (5)
Uneasy feelings about the rightness of an action (6)

Black Boy Vocabulary Word Search 1 Answer Key

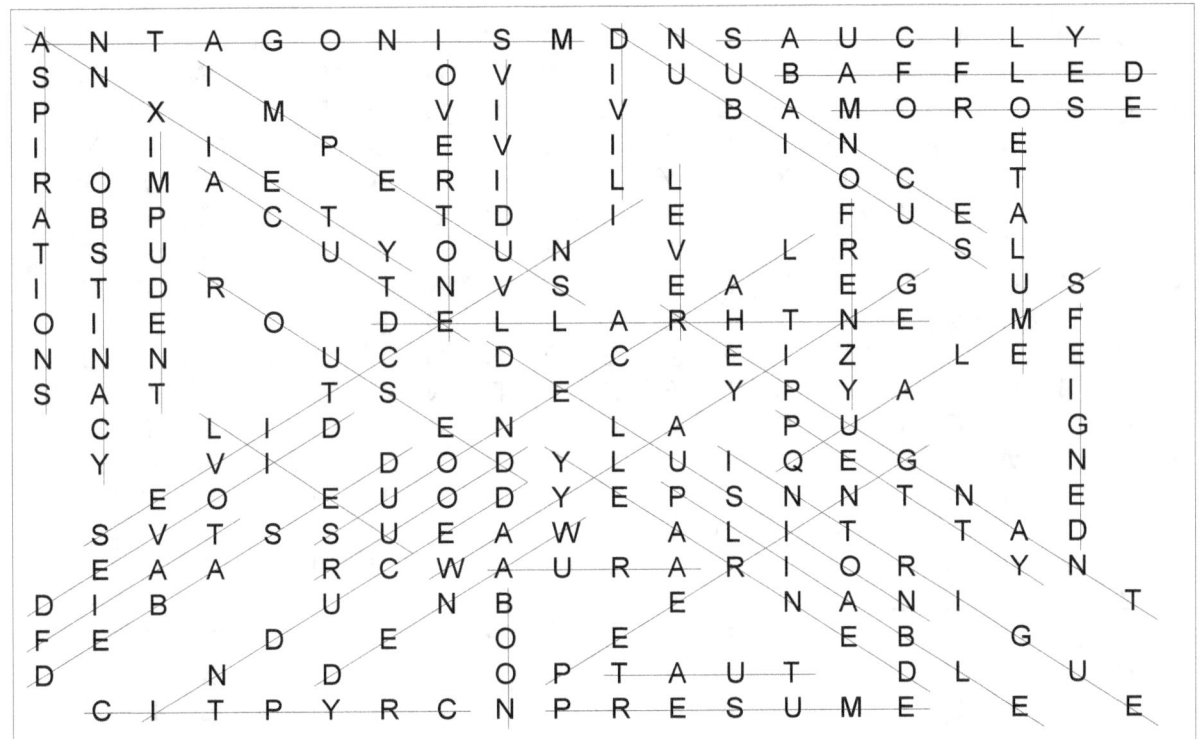

A benefit (4)
A false belief or opinion (8)
A secret or underhanded scheme (8)
A state of uneasiness and apprehension (7)
A state of violent or wild excitement (6)
Abusive language (10)
Ambitions (11)
Ambushing; intercepting someone unexpectedly (9)
An impelling force (7)
An order or authorization (4)
An ulterior meaning or quality; an implication or hint (8)
Approached an end (5)
Atmosphere (4)
Caused (7)
Characterized by theft (9)
Completely lacking or empty (6)
Discolored; showing extreme anger (5)
Disrespectfully (7)
Doubtful (7)
Easily influenced or persuaded (7)
Excited as to anger or action; stirred up (6)
Gave a false appearance of; pretended (7)
Gloomy (6)
Had a strong, often melancholy desire (7)
Heard, seen or felt as if real (5)
Hostility that results in active resistance or oppression (10)
Imitate (7)
In place of (4)
Looking intently or searchingly (7)
Lowered in character, quality or value (7)
Offensive or repulsive (9)
Offensively bold (8)
Puzzled; confused (7)
Sharp or severe; intense (5)
Silently ill-humored or sternly obstinate (4)
Spellbound; captivated (10)
Stubbornness (9)
Subtle or slight degree of difference (6)
Take for granted as being true (7)
Tending to conceal or camouflage (7)
Tight; tense (4)
To take great pleasure or delight (5)
Trivial (5)
Uneasy feelings about the rightness of an action (6)

Black Boy Vocabulary Word Search 2

```
M B D I M P E T U S F Z N F A C U T E J
A X A M D S U H V R I A H D R S D W J C
N R M N E A K D C R A N U G U E E I W B
T C O N T E M P L A T E A R D E N T L Y
A A Y R A E D X N Y C V R O A T G Z Y J
G G N I T E R O K N Q E U Z R P I E Y U
O V Z T S Q O I A Q P R S I A L E V E R
N J X U A B V U N T S U G N S I F I M G
I K O A V M N F I G O U Z C P A L T U L
S R G L E P O T T N E P N O I B S C L C
M L N D D X I U E F X Y F N R L A I A B
K I I S F O Z C N S P Y Q C A E U D T C
D V Y W U W R V Y T L D I E T I C N E Y
E I A S A A E S O R O M N I I N I V G
L D L G L N V S Q L I O C V O D L V I Z
U Y Y P H E X A K C T H U A N U Y T V P
S Z A J E D L I I R E Y R B S C R H I S
I T W X X T S M E L D N R L F E N L D H
O P P B M D T V L T E V E E X D M X H L
N H B S D T O Y K F Y D D E B A S E D N
```

A benefit (4)
A false belief or opinion (8)
A secret or underhanded scheme (8)
A state of uneasiness and apprehension (7)
A state of violent or wild excitement (6)
Acquired (8)
Ambitions (11)
Ambushing; intercepting someone unexpectedly (9)
An impelling force (7)
An order or authorization (4)
An ulterior meaning or quality; an implication or hint (8)
Approached an end (5)
Atmosphere (4)
Caused (7)
Ceremony (6)
Characterized by strong enthusiasm or devotion (8)
Characterized by theft (9)
Destroyed (10)
Discolored; showing extreme anger (5)
Disrespectfully (7)
Easily influenced or persuaded (7)

Equivalent in effect or value (10)
Excited as to anger or action; stirred up (6)
Gave a false appearance of; pretended (7)
Gloomy (6)
Heard, seen or felt as if real (5)
Hostility that results in active resistance or oppression (10)
Imitate (7)
Impossible to comprehend or fully grasp (13)
In place of (4)
Lowered in character, quality or value (7)
Made use of (7)
Made use of selfishly or unethically (9)
Revengeful (10)
Sharp or severe; intense (5)
Silently ill-humored or sternly obstinate (4)
Speaking in a playful or teasing way (9)
Stealthily (15)
Subtle or slight degree of difference (6)
Thing about (11)
Tight; tense (4)
To take great pleasure or delight (5)
Trivial (5)

Black Boy Vocabulary Word Search 2 Answer Key

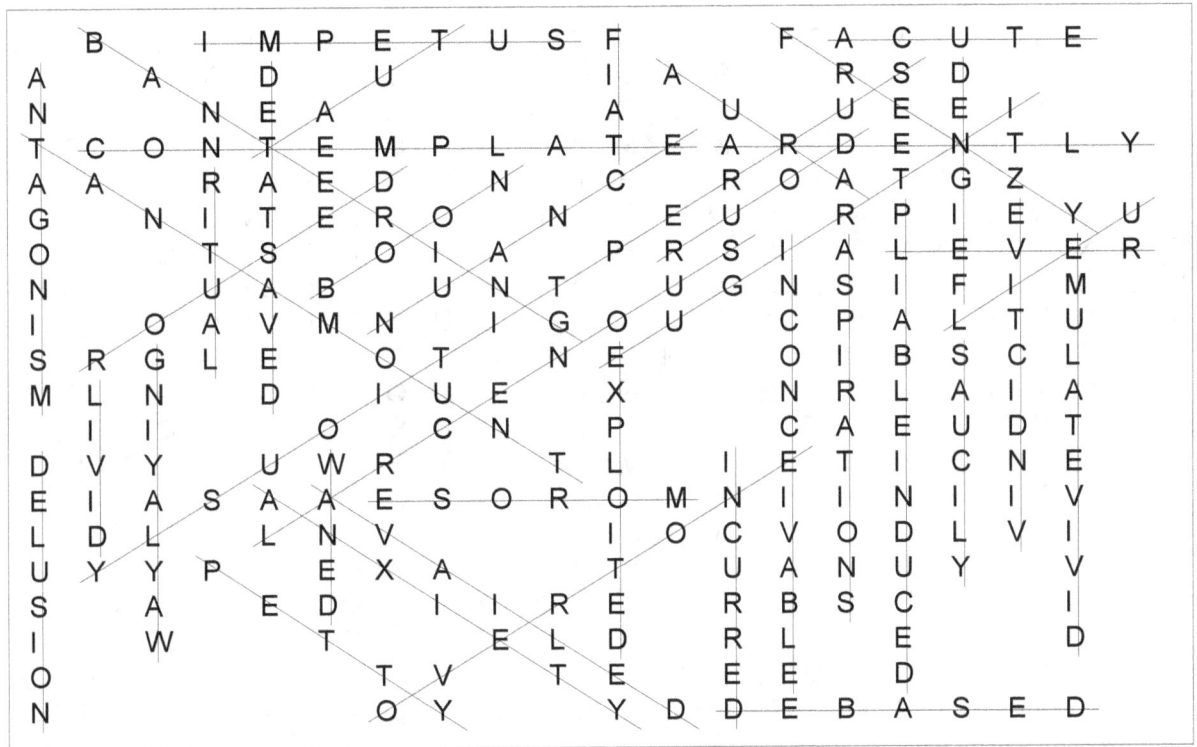

A benefit (4)
A false belief or opinion (8)
A secret or underhanded scheme (8)
A state of uneasiness and apprehension (7)
A state of violent or wild excitement (6)
Acquired (8)
Ambitions (11)
Ambushing; intercepting someone unexpectedly (9)
An impelling force (7)
An order or authorization (4)
An ulterior meaning or quality; an implication or hint (8)
Approached an end (5)
Atmosphere (4)
Caused (7)
Ceremony (6)
Characterized by strong enthusiasm or devotion (8)
Characterized by theft (9)
Destroyed (10)
Discolored; showing extreme anger (5)
Disrespectfully (7)
Easily influenced or persuaded (7)
Equivalent in effect or value (10)
Excited as to anger or action; stirred up (6)
Gave a false appearance of; pretended (7)
Gloomy (6)
Heard, seen or felt as if real (5)
Hostility that results in active resistance or oppression (10)
Imitate (7)
Impossible to comprehend or fully grasp (13)
In place of (4)
Lowered in character, quality or value (7)
Made use of (7)
Made use of selfishly or unethically (9)
Revengeful (10)
Sharp or severe; intense (5)
Silently ill-humored or sternly obstinate (4)
Speaking in a playful or teasing way (9)
Stealthily (15)
Subtle or slight degree of difference (6)
Thing about (11)
Tight; tense (4)
To take great pleasure or delight (5)
Trivial (5)

Black Boy Vocabulary Word Search 3

```
T J T Q J X J O D E V A S T A T E D E C U D N I M
A T L M Y V V B E X P L O I T E D S Y L X S H L C
N Y A N L D G S F W T E R J N D A R C Y U F T T P
T M R K T R Q T G Y K M M W A U F E N O T R E V O
A E C S N N D I L N G U H W N V L R U V D R L V J
M H E Q E V V N W Q M S P T G H N T E L W E J I H
O P N F D Q N A B I I E E D U V P Z I N V M D V N
U S O C R U Y C Z N M R K D P M D E R E Z I E I O
N A U R A L S Y T T E P S D E S U O R N V Y R D I
T L S N A P E R K D E M E T R L L P O I L T R E T
P B C Y X A I R N E L N N T X A U O L T Y E U B C
A E I D R G W T R A A O T G U S B S N L Y I C A E
I N D N U F K I U W C L V Q F S T E I M T X N S L
G P E E O B N Q E L A S S I T G G C M O K N I E I
L D L K D G I T L U A K A H S L U R P R N A Q D D
A Y F C T F A O T J D T V C U A M Y U O A C K I E
T F F J A L L I U T N V E D S Q C P D S W C O K R
S S A V U B R R D S D E N G I E F T E E M V U V P
O X B M T I N T U I T I V E L Y C I N L E W T T M
N S E V I T C E V N I V Y L X X X C T D K M Z N E
```

ACUTE	FIAT	PETTY
ANXIETY	FRENZY	PREDILECTION
ARDENTLY	IMPETUS	PRESUME
AURA	IMPUDENT	QUALMS
BAFFLED	INCURRED	REPUGNANT
BLASPHEMY	INDUCED	REVEL
BOON	INDULGENTLY	RITUAL
CAPITULATE	INTRIGUE	ROUSED
CONTEMPTUOUS	INTUITIVELY	SAUCILY
CRYPTIC	INVECTIVES	SAUNTERED
DEBASED	LARCENOUS	SQUALOR
DELUSION	LIEU	TANTAMOUNT
DEVASTATED	LIVID	TAUT
DEVOID	MOROSE	VIVID
DOUR	NOSTALGIA	WANED
DUBIOUS	NUANCE	WAYLAYING
EMULATE	OBSTINACY	YEARNED
EXPLOITED	OVERTONE	
FEIGNED	PEERING	

Black Boy Vocabulary Word Search 3 Answer Key

ACUTE	FIAT	PETTY
ANXIETY	FRENZY	PREDILECTION
ARDENTLY	IMPETUS	PRESUME
AURA	IMPUDENT	QUALMS
BAFFLED	INCURRED	REPUGNANT
BLASPHEMY	INDUCED	REVEL
BOON	INDULGENTLY	RITUAL
CAPITULATE	INTRIGUE	ROUSED
CONTEMPTUOUS	INTUITIVELY	SAUCILY
CRYPTIC	INVECTIVES	SAUNTERED
DEBASED	LARCENOUS	SQUALOR
DELUSION	LIEU	TANTAMOUNT
DEVASTATED	LIVID	TAUT
DEVOID	MOROSE	VIVID
DOUR	NOSTALGIA	WANED
DUBIOUS	NUANCE	WAYLAYING
EMULATE	OBSTINACY	YEARNED
EXPLOITED	OVERTONE	
FEIGNED	PEERING	

Black Boy Vocabulary Word Search 4

```
D I S S E M B L E T I D N O C E R M C R Y P T I C
E A Q Y C O N T E M P T U O U S S T W Z D R T F W
C I H T N I M P U D E N T C Q I O W G M E E E D G
U G C I E J R D E J D H D H N R B V Q M V S U M J
D L P R I R Y N E E J E J O P S E W E P A U G F C
N A M A V F A E L L R C G S Q D M L S R S M I E Y
I T X D R W N F A E U A R F S E U M F O T E R I S
T S R I E T F V T R T S W O I B L N S V A O T G M
I O V L S A P N Z N N P I Y U A A U Z O T H N N J
D N O O B Y U L A R C E N O U S T K Y C E L I E U
O U T S U A I R I V I T D Q N E E T G A D R S D D
U A B U S V N F A A C T L S P D E D G T R O A U V
R N R I I T S T P Q B Y U M F I Z T D I R B V T V
D C P D O T P Q E N Z L I A X W J L N O M S A I Q
E E F E E U I C U R M L E N L S E C M N C T I C V
V E R Q E N S V H A I X A F S V U K V S P I L I T
O T A U T R T D E W L N Q Z E R V I V I D N E L M
I U S A U C I L Y L Y O G R R X G S V X T A D O W
D C V W R H G N Y S Y Y R E P U G N A N T C J S B
L A F R E N Z Y G P R E D I L E C T I O N Y Z H P
```

ACUTE	FIAT	PRESUME
ANTAGONISM	FRENZY	PROVOCATIONS
ANXIETY	IMPETUS	QUALMS
ARDENTLY	IMPUDENT	RECONDITE
AURA	INCURRED	REPUGNANT
AVAILED	INDUCED	REVEL
BAFFLED	INTRIGUE	RITUAL
BANTERING	INTUITIVELY	ROUSED
BOON	LARCENOUS	SAUCILY
CONTEMPTUOUS	LIEU	SAUNTERED
CRYPTIC	LIVID	SOLICITUDE
DEBASED	MOROSE	SOLIDARITY
DELUSION	NOSTALGIA	SQUALOR
DEVASTATED	NUANCE	SUBSERVIENCE
DEVOID	OBSTINACY	TAUT
DISSEMBLE	OVERTONE	VIVID
DOUR	PEERING	WANED
DUBIOUS	PETTY	YEARNED
EMULATE	PLIABLE	
FEIGNED	PREDILECTION	

Black Boy Vocabulary Word Search 4 Answer Key

ACUTE	FIAT	PRESUME
ANTAGONISM	FRENZY	PROVOCATIONS
ANXIETY	IMPETUS	QUALMS
ARDENTLY	IMPUDENT	RECONDITE
AURA	INCURRED	REPUGNANT
AVAILED	INDUCED	REVEL
BAFFLED	INTRIGUE	RITUAL
BANTERING	INTUITIVELY	ROUSED
BOON	LARCENOUS	SAUCILY
CONTEMPTUOUS	LIEU	SAUNTERED
CRYPTIC	LIVID	SOLICITUDE
DEBASED	MOROSE	SOLIDARITY
DELUSION	NOSTALGIA	SQUALOR
DEVASTATED	NUANCE	SUBSERVIENCE
DEVOID	OBSTINACY	TAUT
DISSEMBLE	OVERTONE	VIVID
DOUR	PEERING	WANED
DUBIOUS	PETTY	YEARNED
EMULATE	PLIABLE	
FEIGNED	PREDILECTION	

Black Boy Vocabulary Crossword 1

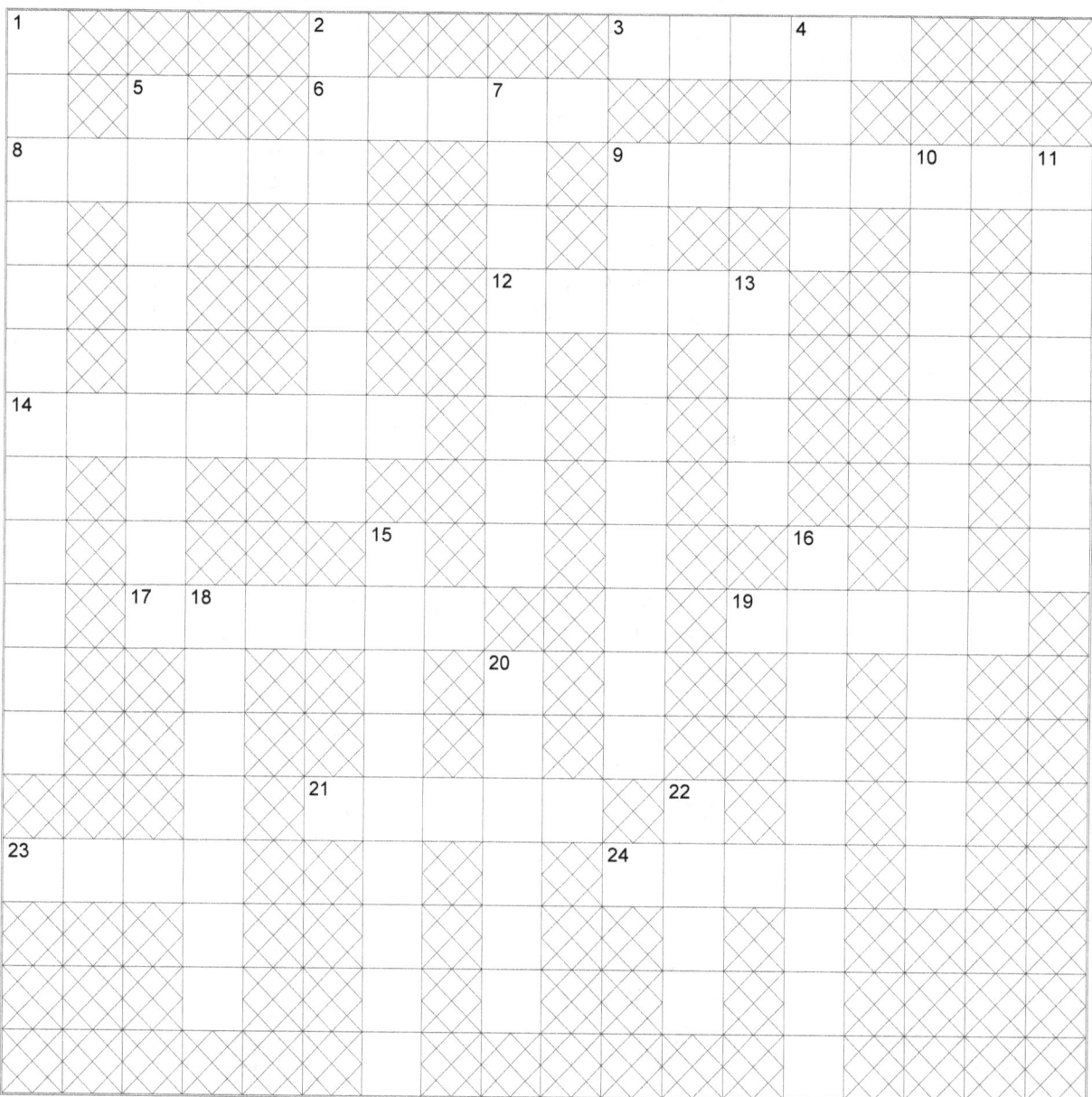

Across
3. Sharp or severe; intense
6. Heard, seen or felt as if real
8. Subtle or slight degree of difference
9. Acquired
12. To take great pleasure or delight
14. Looking intently or searchingly
17. Completely lacking or empty
19. Approached an end
21. Trivial
23. Atmosphere
24. Silently ill-humored or sternly obstinate

Down
1. Scornful
2. An ulterior meaning or quality; an implication or hint
4. Tight; tense
5. Strolled
7. A secret or underhanded scheme
9. Abusive language
10. Steadily; persistently
11. Doubtful
13. In place of
15. To disguise one's real nature, motives or feelings
16. Speaking in a playful or teasing way
18. Imitate
20. Ceremony
22. A benefit

Black Boy Vocabulary Crossword 1 Answer Key

	1 C				2 O				3 A	C	U	4 T	E		
	O		5 S		6 V	I	V	7 I	D			A			
8 N	U	A	N	C	E			N		9 I	N	C	U	R	R	E	10 R	11 D
	T		U		R			T		N			T		E		U
	E		N		T		12 R	E	V	13 E	L			L		B
	M		T		O		I			E		I			E		I
14 P	E	E	R	I	N	G		G		C		E			N		O
	T		R		E			U		T		U			T		U
	U		E			15 D		E		I		16 B			L		S
	O		17 D	18 E	V	O	I	D		V		W	A	N	E	D	
	U			M		S		20 R		E		A			S		
	S			U		S		I		S		T			S		
				L		21 P	E	T	T	Y		22 B		E		L
23 A	U	R	A			M		U		24 D	O	U	R			Y
			T			B		A		O		I				
			E			L		L		N		N				
						E						G				

Across
3. Sharp or severe; intense
6. Heard, seen or felt as if real
8. Subtle or slight degree of difference
9. Acquired
12. To take great pleasure or delight
14. Looking intently or searchingly
17. Completely lacking or empty
19. Approached an end
21. Trivial
23. Atmosphere
24. Silently ill-humored or sternly obstinate

Down
1. Scornful
2. An ulterior meaning or quality; an implication or hint
4. Tight; tense
5. Strolled
7. A secret or underhanded scheme
9. Abusive language
10. Steadily; persistently
11. Doubtful
13. In place of
15. To disguise one's real nature, motives or feelings
16. Speaking in a playful or teasing way
18. Imitate
20. Ceremony
22. A benefit

Black Boy Vocabulary Crossword 2

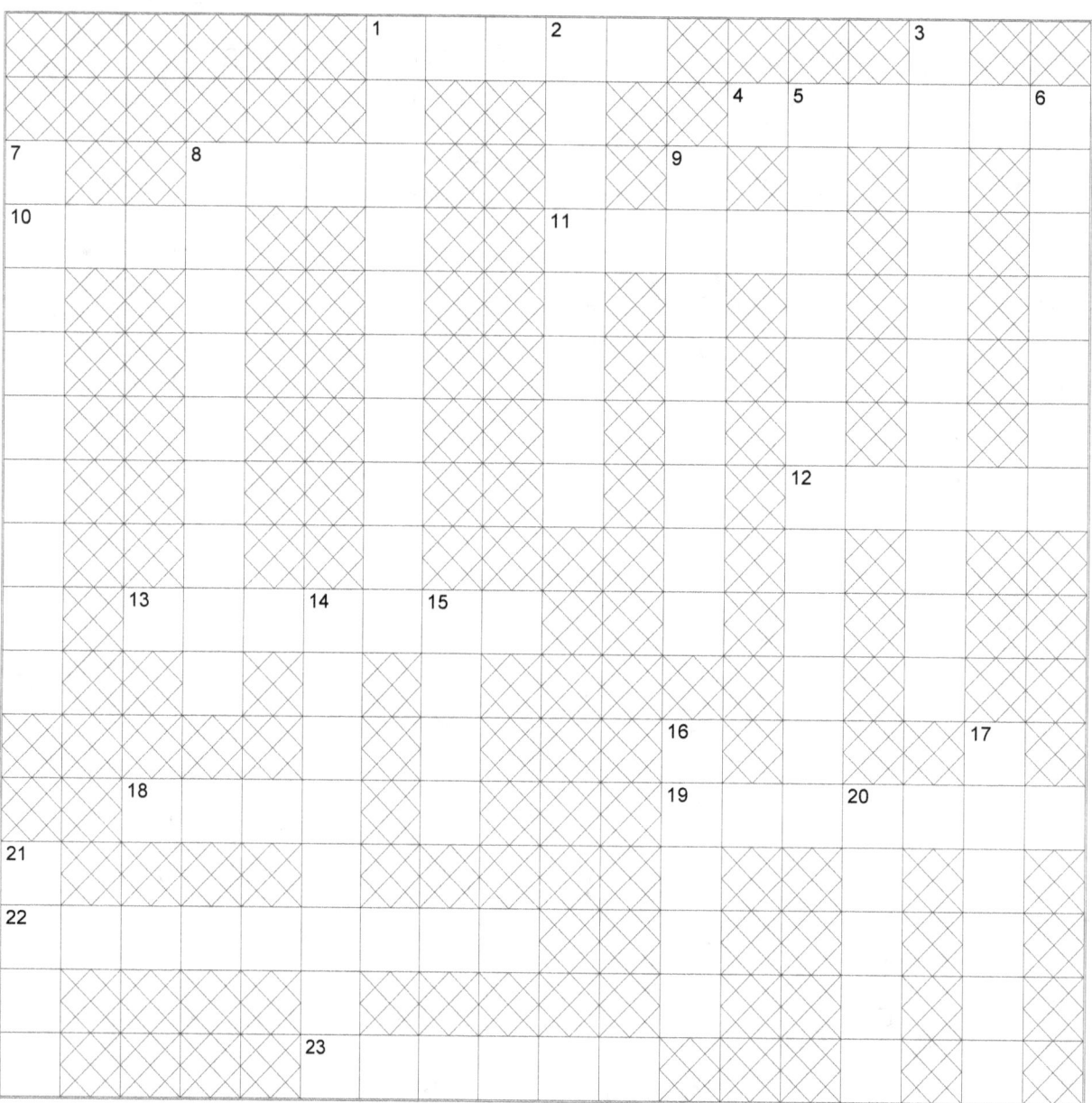

Across
1. Heard, seen or felt as if real
4. A state of violent or wild excitement
8. A benefit
10. Atmosphere
11. To take great pleasure or delight
12. Discolored; showing extreme anger
13. A state of uneasiness and apprehension
18. In place of
19. Tending to conceal or camouflage
22. Making an earnest appeal
23. Completely lacking or empty

Down
1. Revengeful
2. A secret or underhanded scheme
3. Without the use of rational reasoning; instinctively
5. Steadily; persistently
6. Had a strong, often melancholy desire
7. Strolled
8. Speaking in a playful or teasing way
9. An ulterior meaning or quality; an implication or hint
14. Acquired
15. Tight; tense
16. Sharp or severe; intense
17. Ceremony
20. Trivial
21. An order or authorization

Black Boy Vocabulary Crossword 2 Answer Key

Across
1. Heard, seen or felt as if real
4. A state of violent or wild excitement
8. A benefit
10. Atmosphere
11. To take great pleasure or delight
12. Discolored; showing extreme anger
13. A state of uneasiness and apprehension
18. In place of
19. Tending to conceal or camouflage
22. Making an earnest appeal
23. Completely lacking or empty

Down
1. Revengeful
2. A secret or underhanded scheme
3. Without the use of rational reasoning; instinctively
5. Steadily; persistently
6. Had a strong, often melancholy desire
7. Strolled
8. Speaking in a playful or teasing way
9. An ulterior meaning or quality; an implication or hint
14. Acquired
15. Tight; tense
16. Sharp or severe; intense
17. Ceremony
20. Trivial
21. An order or authorization

Answers filled in grid:
- 1A VIVID
- 4A FRENZY
- 7D SAUNTERED
- 8A BOON
- 8D BANTERING
- 10A AURA
- 11A REVEL
- 1D VINDICTIVE
- 2D INTRIGUE
- 3D INTUITIVELY
- 5D RELENTLESSLY
- 6D YEARNED
- 9D OVERTONES
- 12A LIVID
- 13A ANXIETY
- 14D INCURRED
- 15D TAUT
- 16D ACUTE
- 17D RITE
- 18A LIEU
- 19A CRYPTIC
- 20D PETTY
- 21D FIAT
- 22A IMPLORING
- 23A DEVOID

Black Boy Vocabulary Crossword 3

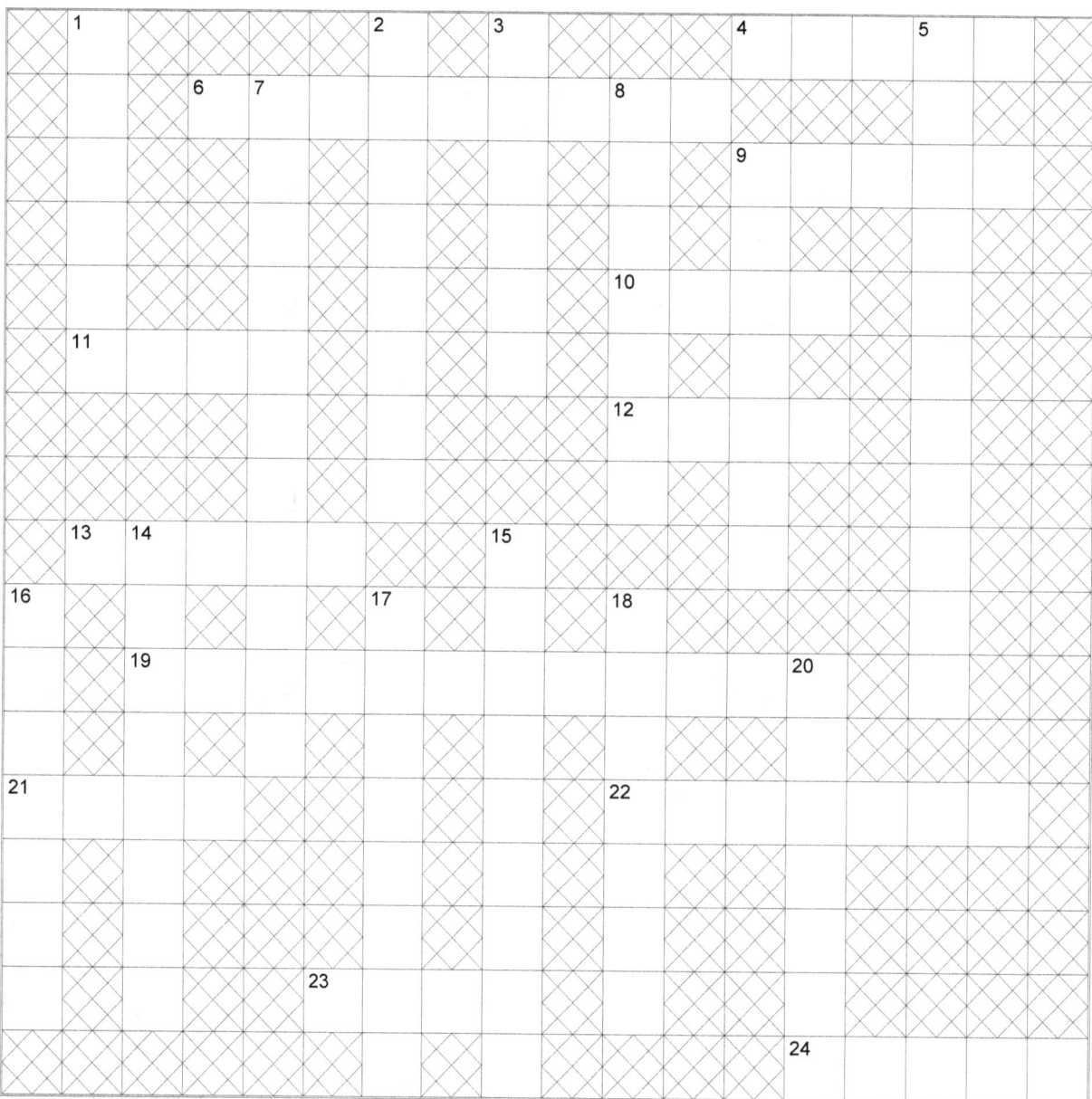

Across
4. Discolored; showing extreme anger
6. Strolled
9. Trivial
10. In place of
11. Silently ill-humored or sternly obstinate
12. Tight; tense
13. Heard, seen or felt as if real
19. Scornful
21. Atmosphere
22. Caused
23. A benefit
24. To take great pleasure or delight

Down
1. Excited as to anger or action; stirred up
2. A secret or underhanded scheme
3. Completely lacking or empty
5. Without the use of rational reasoning; instinctively
7. Ambitions
8. Imitate
9. Take for granted as being true
14. Acquired
15. Making an earnest appeal
16. Easily influenced or persuaded
17. A false belief or opinion
18. Doubtful
20. A filthy and wretched condition

Black Boy Vocabulary Crossword 3 Answer Key

	1 R				2 I		3 D			4 L	I	V	5 I	D	
	O		6 S	7 A	U	N	T	E	R	8 E	D		N		
	U			S		T		V		M		9 P	E	T	T	Y
	S			P		R		O		U		R		U	
	E			I		I		I		10 L	I	E	U		I
	11 D	O	U	R		G		D		A		S		T
				A		U				12 T	A	U	T		I
				T		E				E		M			V
	13 V	14 I	V	I	D			15 I			E			E
16 P		N		O		17 D		M		18 D				L
L		19 C	O	N	T	E	M	P	T	U	O	U	20 S		Y
I		U		S		L		L		B		Q	
21 A	U	R	A		U		O		22 I	N	D	U	C	E	D
B		R			S		R		O		A		
L		E			I		I		U		L		
E		D		23 B	O	O	N		S		O		
				N		G		24 R	E	V	E	L	

Across
4. Discolored; showing extreme anger
6. Strolled
9. Trivial
10. In place of
11. Silently ill-humored or sternly obstinate
12. Tight; tense
13. Heard, seen or felt as if real
19. Scornful
21. Atmosphere
22. Caused
23. A benefit
24. To take great pleasure or delight

Down
1. Excited as to anger or action; stirred up
2. A secret or underhanded scheme
3. Completely lacking or empty
5. Without the use of rational reasoning; instinctively
7. Ambitions
8. Imitate
9. Take for granted as being true
14. Acquired
15. Making an earnest appeal
16. Easily influenced or persuaded
17. A false belief or opinion
18. Doubtful
20. A filthy and wretched condition

Black Boy Vocabulary Crossword 4

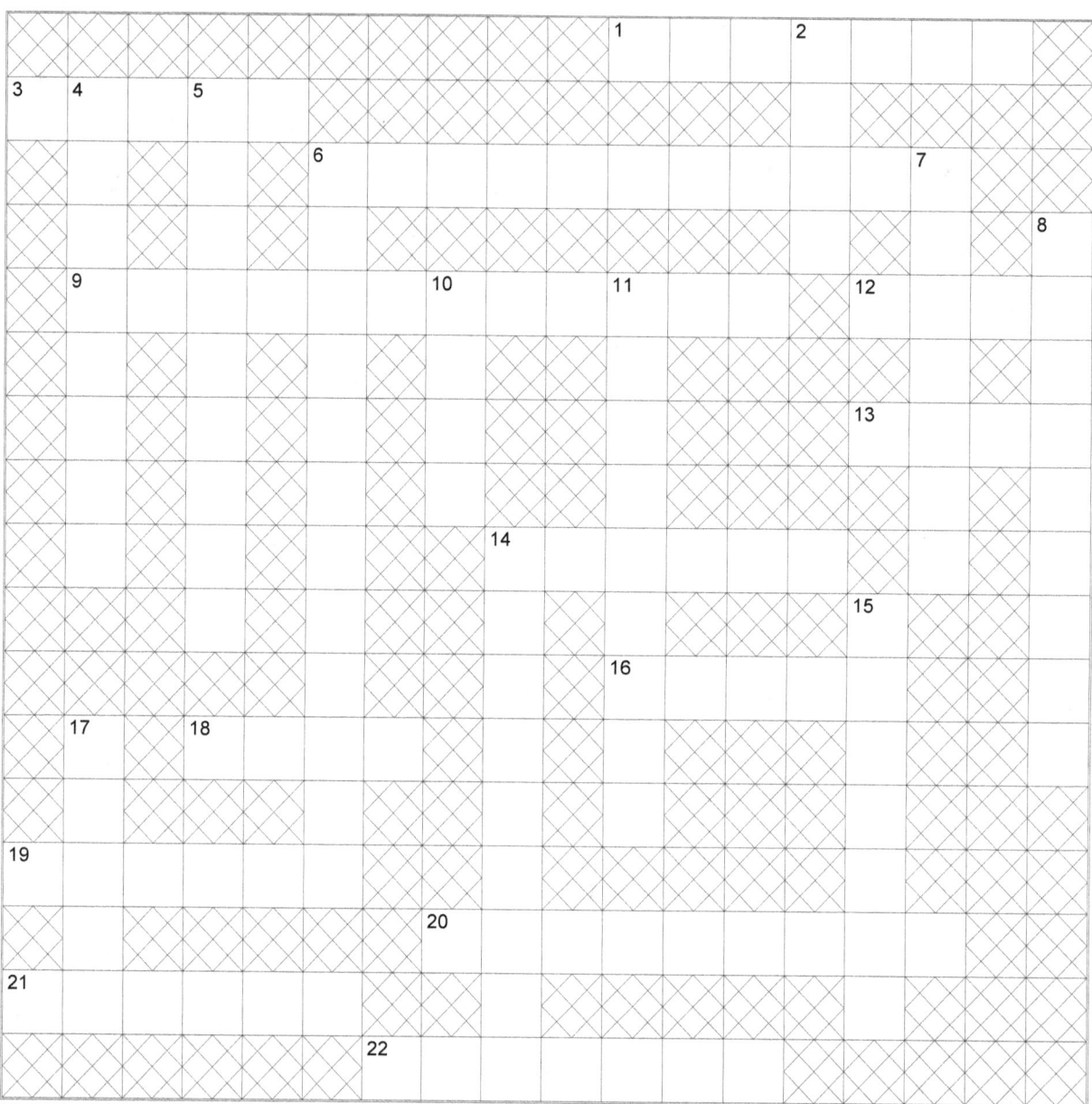

Across
1. Puzzled; confused
3. Heard, seen or felt as if real
6. Thing about
9. Steadily; persistently
12. Atmosphere
13. Tight; tense
14. Ceremony
16. To take great pleasure or delight
18. A benefit
19. Uneasy feelings about the rightness of an action
20. To disguise one's real nature, motives or feelings
21. Completely lacking or empty
22. Take for granted as being true

Down
2. An order or authorization
4. A secret or underhanded scheme
5. Making an earnest appeal
6. Scornful
7. Imitate
8. Speaking in a playful or teasing way
10. In place of
11. Strolled
14. Not easily understood
15. Easily influenced or persuaded
17. Sharp or severe; intense

Black Boy Vocabulary Crossword 4 Answer Key

							¹B	A	F	²F	L	E	D	
³V	⁴I	⁵V	I	D						I		⁷		
	N	M		⁶C	O	N	T	E	M	P	L	A	T	E
	T	P		O						T		M		⁸B
	⁹R	E	L	E	N	¹⁰T	E	¹¹S	L	Y		¹²A	U	R	A
	I		O		T		I		A				L		N
	G		R		E		E		U			¹³T	A	U	T
	U		I		M		U		N				T		E
	E		N		P		¹⁴R	I	T	U	A	L		E		R
			G		T			E				¹⁵P			I
					U			C		¹⁶R	E	V	E	L		N
	¹⁷A		¹⁸B	O	O	N		O		E			I			G
	C			U				N		D			A			
¹⁹Q	U	A	L	M	S			D					B			
	T					²⁰D	I	S	S	E	M	B	L	E		
²¹D	E	V	O	I	D		T						E			
					²²P	R	E	S	U	M	E					

Across
1. Puzzled; confused
3. Heard, seen or felt as if real
6. Thing about
9. Steadily; persistently
12. Atmosphere
13. Tight; tense
14. Ceremony
16. To take great pleasure or delight
18. A benefit
19. Uneasy feelings about the rightness of an action
20. To disguise one's real nature, motives or feelings
21. Completely lacking or empty
22. Take for granted as being true

Down
2. An order or authorization
4. A secret or underhanded scheme
5. Making an earnest appeal
6. Scornful
7. Imitate
8. Speaking in a playful or teasing way
10. In place of
11. Strolled
14. Not easily understood
15. Easily influenced or persuaded
17. Sharp or severe; intense

Black Boy Vocabulary Juggle Letters 1

1. ENNUAC = 1. _____
   Subtle or slight degree of difference

2. RONZTIPGANI = 2. _____
   Going to as a customer

3. PUNTEANRG = 3. _____
   Offensive or repulsive

4. ASIGLOATN = 4. _____
   A bittersweet longing for things of the past

5. GEIENRP = 5. _____
   Looking intently or searchingly

6. AUTDNENNIICO = 6. _____
   Public condemnation or censure

7. FRZENY = 7. _____
   A state of violent or wild excitement

8. TLDRAYEN = 8. _____
   Characterized by strong enthusiasm or devotion

9. NTIRNAEGB = 9. _____
   Speaking in a playful or teasing way

10. CSVNBISEUEER =10. _____
    Being subordinate; of a lesser position

11. ROUD =11. _____
    Silently ill-humored or sternly obstinate

12. YRESTLNEELLS =12. _____
    Steadily; persistently

13. UOUCPLNSIYCSO =13. _____
    Obviously

14. LEMAUTE =14. _____
    Imitate

15. NEAUETDRS =15. _____
    Strolled

Black Boy Vocabulary Juggle Letters 1 Answer Key

1. ENNUAC = 1. NUANCE
   Subtle or slight degree of difference

2. RONZTIPGANI = 2. PATRONIZING
   Going to as a customer

3. PUNTEANRG = 3. REPUGNANT
   Offensive or repulsive

4. ASIGLOATN = 4. NOSTALGIA
   A bittersweet longing for things of the past

5. GEIENRP = 5. PEERING
   Looking intently or searchingly

6. AUTDNENNIICO = 6. DENUNCIATION
   Public condemnation or censure

7. FRZENY = 7. FRENZY
   A state of violent or wild excitement

8. TLDRAYEN = 8. ARDENTLY
   Characterized by strong enthusiasm or devotion

9. NTIRNAEGB = 9. BANTERING
   Speaking in a playful or teasing way

10. CSVNBISEUEER = 10. SUBSERVIENCE
    Being subordinate; of a lesser position

11. ROUD = 11. DOUR
    Silently ill-humored or sternly obstinate

12. YRESTLNEELLS = 12. RELENTLESSLY
    Steadily; persistently

13. UOUCPLNSIYCSO = 13. CONSPICUOUSLY
    Obviously

14. LEMAUTE = 14. EMULATE
    Imitate

15. NEAUETDRS = 15. SAUNTERED
    Strolled

Black Boy Vocabulary Juggle Letters 2

1. VOEDDI = 1. _____
   Completely lacking or empty

2. TALEEUM = 2. _____
   Imitate

3. VENVSECTII = 3. _____
   Abusive language

4. EUPESRM = 4. _____
   Take for granted as being true

5. EENIGDF = 5. _____
   Gave a false appearance of; pretended

6. DDEEBSA = 6. _____
   Lowered in character, quality or value

7. PEUISTM = 7. _____
   An impelling force

8. EILU = 8. _____
   In place of

9. TYELNLESLERS = 9. _____
   Steadily; persistently

10. NTULEIIITVY = 10. _____
    Without the use of rational reasoning; instinctively

11. ITYRCPC = 11. _____
    Tending to conceal or camouflage

12. LAILBCPAME = 12. _____
    Impossible to please or satisfy

13. LNATETOMPCE = 13. _____
    Thing about

14. XTEYNIA = 14. _____
    A state of uneasiness and apprehension

15. TSRTOSUPIYELIUR = 15. _____
    Stealthily

Black Boy Vocabulary Juggle Letters 2 Answer Key

1. VOEDDI = 1. DEVOID
   Completely lacking or empty

2. TALEEUM = 2. EMULATE
   Imitate

3. VENVSECTII = 3. INVECTIVES
   Abusive language

4. EUPESRM = 4. PRESUME
   Take for granted as being true

5. EENIGDF = 5. FEIGNED
   Gave a false appearance of; pretended

6. DDEEBSA = 6. DEBASED
   Lowered in character, quality or value

7. PEUISTM = 7. IMPETUS
   An impelling force

8. EILU = 8. LIEU
   In place of

9. TYELNLESLERS = 9. RELENTLESSLY
   Steadily; persistently

10. NTULEIIITVY = 10. INTUITIVELY
    Without the use of rational reasoning; instinctively

11. ITYRCPC = 11. CRYPTIC
    Tending to conceal or camouflage

12. LAILBCPAME = 12. IMPLACABLE
    Impossible to please or satisfy

13. LNATETOMPCE = 13. CONTEMPLATE
    Thing about

14. XTEYNIA = 14. ANXIETY
    A state of uneasiness and apprehension

15. TSRTOSUPIYELIUR = 15. SURREPTITIOUSLY
    Stealthily

Black Boy Vocabulary Juggle Letters 3

1. LEEVR = 1. _____
   To take great pleasure or delight

2. VDIIL = 2. _____
   Discolored; showing extreme anger

3. ITRGOILEN = 3. _____
   Standing idly about; lingering with no purpose

4. INAONPIRZGT = 4. _____
   Going to as a customer

5. URPEMSE = 5. _____
   Take for granted as being true

6. ERNRCUDI = 6. _____
   Acquired

7. PGERNUTNA = 7. _____
   Offensive or repulsive

8. RITEUIGN = 8. _____
   A secret or underhanded scheme

9. SAUYLCI = 9. _____
   Disrespectfully

10. AMOSAGINNT =10. _____
    Hostility that results in active resistance or oppression

11. ULIE =11. _____
    In place of

12. MTEAELU =12. _____
    Imitate

13. POIRYISUTETSRLU =13. _____
    Stealthily

14. NGOIMILPR =14. _____
    Making an earnest appeal

15. CCTYPRI =15. _____
    Tending to conceal or camouflage

Black Boy Vocabulary Juggle Letters 3 Answer Key

1. LEEVR = 1. REVEL
To take great pleasure or delight

2. VDIIL = 2. LIVID
Discolored; showing extreme anger

3. ITRGOILEN = 3. LOITERING
Standing idly about; lingering with no purpose

4. INAONPIRZGT = 4. PATRONIZING
Going to as a customer

5. URPEMSE = 5. PRESUME
Take for granted as being true

6. ERNRCUDI = 6. INCURRED
Acquired

7. PGERNUTNA = 7. REPUGNANT
Offensive or repulsive

8. RITEUIGN = 8. INTRIGUE
A secret or underhanded scheme

9. SAUYLCI = 9. SAUCILY
Disrespectfully

10. AMOSAGINNT =10. ANTAGONISM
Hostility that results in active resistance or oppression

11. ULIE =11. LIEU
In place of

12. MTEAELU =12. EMULATE
Imitate

13. POIRYISUTETSRLU =13. SURREPTITIOUSLY
Stealthily

14. NGOIMILPR =14. IMPLORING
Making an earnest appeal

15. CCTYPRI =15. CRYPTIC
Tending to conceal or camouflage

Black Boy Vocabulary Juggle Letters 4

1. YRITEULSSRUTOIP = 1. _____
   Stealthily

2. DIEEITPLCNRO = 2. _____
   Preference

3. LTECISDOUI = 3. _____
   Care or concern for the well-being of another

4. NNOCIEBAICLVE = 4. _____
   Impossible to comprehend or fully grasp

5. IOUBDUS = 5. _____
   Doubtful

6. LEPTEIDXO = 6. _____
   Made use of selfishly or unethically

7. PSMETUI = 7. _____
   An impelling force

8. ITOUNCINDANE = 8. _____
   Public condemnation or censure

9. CYRCPTI = 9. _____
   Tending to conceal or camouflage

10. TEACU =10. _____
    Sharp or severe; intense

11. EALBAIMPCL =11. _____
    Impossible to please or satisfy

12. CEDUNID =12. _____
    Caused

13. ULAOERNSC =13. _____
    Characterized by theft

14. SNOLSOUIUCCPY =14. _____
    Obviously

15. NUAOTMATNT =15. _____
    Equivalent in effect or value

Copyrighted

Black Boy Vocabulary Juggle Letters 4 Answer Key

1. YRITEULSSRUTOIP = 1. SURREPTITIOUSLY
Stealthily

2. DIEEITPLCNRO = 2. PREDILECTION
Preference

3. LTECISDOUI = 3. SOLICITUDE
Care or concern for the well-being of another

4. NNOCIEBAICLVE = 4. INCONCEIVABLE
Impossible to comprehend or fully grasp

5. IOUBDUS = 5. DUBIOUS
Doubtful

6. LEPTEIDXO = 6. EXPLOITED
Made use of selfishly or unethically

7. PSMETUI = 7. IMPETUS
An impelling force

8. ITOUNCINDANE = 8. DENUNCIATION
Public condemnation or censure

9. CYRCPTI = 9. CRYPTIC
Tending to conceal or camouflage

10. TEACU = 10. ACUTE
Sharp or severe; intense

11. EALBAIMPCL = 11. IMPLACABLE
Impossible to please or satisfy

12. CEDUNID = 12. INDUCED
Caused

13. ULAOERNSC = 13. LARCENOUS
Characterized by theft

14. SNOLSOUIUCCPY = 14. CONSPICUOUSLY
Obviously

15. NUAOTMATNT = 15. TANTAMOUNT
Equivalent in effect or value

ACUTE	Sharp or severe; intense
ANTAGONISM	Hostility that results in active resistance or oppression
ANXIETY	A state of uneasiness and apprehension
ARDENTLY	Characterized by strong enthusiasm or devotion
ASPIRATIONS	Ambitions
AURA	Atmosphere

AVAILED	Made use of
BAFFLED	Puzzled; confused
BANTERING	Speaking in a playful or teasing way
BLASPHEMY	To speak of God in an irreverent manner
BOON	A benefit
CAPITULATE	Surrender; give up

CONSPICUOUSLY	Obviously
CONTEMPLATE	Thing about
CONTEMPTUOUS	Scornful
CRYPTIC	Tending to conceal or camouflage
DEBASED	Lowered in character, quality or value
DELUSION	A false belief or opinion

DENUNCIATION	Public condemnation or censure
DEVASTATED	Destroyed
DEVOID	Completely lacking or empty
DISSEMBLE	To disguise one's real nature, motives or feelings
DOUR	Silently ill-humored or sternly obstinate
DUBIOUS	Doubtful

EMULATE	Imitate
ENTHRALLED	Spellbound; captivated
EXPLOITED	Made use of selfishly or unethically
FEIGNED	Gave a false appearance of; pretended
FIAT	An order or authorization
FRENZY	A state of violent or wild excitement

HYPOTHETICAL	Suppositional
IMPETUS	An impelling force
IMPLACABLE	Impossible to please or satisfy
IMPLORING	Making an earnest appeal
IMPUDENT	Offensively bold
INCONCEIVABLE	Impossible to comprehend or fully grasp

INCRIMINATING	Causing to appear guilty of a crime or fault
INCURRED	Acquired
INDUCED	Caused
INDULGENTLY	Leniently; patiently
INTRIGUE	A secret or underhanded scheme
INTUITIVELY	Without the use of rational reasoning; instinctively

INVECTIVES	Abusive language
LARCENOUS	Characterized by theft
LIEU	In place of
LIVID	Discolored; showing extreme anger
LOITERING	Standing idly about; lingering with no purpose
MOROSE	Gloomy

NONCHALANTLY	Seeming to be coolly unconcerned or indifferent
NOSTALGIA	A bittersweet longing for things of the past
NUANCE	Subtle or slight degree of difference
OBSTINACY	Stubbornness
OVERTONE	An ulterior meaning or quality; an implication or hint
PATRONIZING	Going to as a customer

PEERING	Looking intently or searchingly
PETTY	Trivial
PLIABLE	Easily influenced or persuaded
PREDILECTION	Preference
PRESUME	Take for granted as being true
PROVOCATIONS	Something that incites or is intended to cause trouble

QUALMS	Uneasy feelings about the rightness of an action
RECONDITE	Not easily understood
RELENTLESSLY	Steadily; persistently
REPUGNANT	Offensive or repulsive
REVEL	To take great pleasure or delight
RITUAL	Ceremony

ROUSED	Excited as to anger or action; stirred up
SAUCILY	Disrespectfully
SAUNTERED	Strolled
SOLICITUDE	Care or concern for the well-being of another
SOLIDARITY	A union of interests or purposes among group members
SQUALOR	A filthy and wretched condition

SUBSERVIENCE	Being subordinate; of a lesser position
SURREPTITIOUSLY	Stealthily
TANTAMOUNT	Equivalent in effect or value
TAUT	Tight; tense
VINDICTIVE	Revengeful
VIVID	Heard, seen or felt as if real

WANED	Approached an end
WAYLAYING	Ambushing; intercepting someone unexpectedly
YEARNED	Had a strong, often melancholy desire

Black Boy Vocabulary

PRESUME	MOROSE	HYPOTHETICAL	INTUITIVELY	FEIGNED
ENTHRALLED	TAUT	REVEL	CONTEMPTUOUS	BANTERING
INTRIGUE	PROVOCATIONS	FREE SPACE	BAFFLED	IMPETUS
ACUTE	ROUSED	CAPITULATE	EMULATE	DELUSION
CRYPTIC	PETTY	SOLIDARITY	IMPUDENT	NOSTALGIA

Black Boy Vocabulary

DENUNCIATION	RECONDITE	DOUR	WANED	INCONCEIVABLE
INCRIMINATING	DEBASED	AURA	VINDICTIVE	SQUALOR
AVAILED	OBSTINACY	FREE SPACE	LIEU	EXPLOITED
SUBSERVIENCE	LOITERING	PATRONIZING	ANTAGONISM	NONCHALANTLY
RELENTLESSLY	DEVASTATED	TANTAMOUNT	DUBIOUS	IMPLACABLE

Black Boy Vocabulary

DEBASED	MOROSE	ACUTE	PROVOCATIONS	BOON
ANXIETY	PETTY	BLASPHEMY	NOSTALGIA	EXPLOITED
IMPLORING	IMPUDENT	FREE SPACE	AURA	LIEU
INDUCED	DEVOID	ROUSED	TANTAMOUNT	CAPITULATE
VIVID	BANTERING	INCONCEIVABLE	SURREPTITIOUSLY	CONSPICUOUSLY

Black Boy Vocabulary

PREDILECTION	PRESUME	INTUITIVELY	CRYPTIC	HYPOTHETICAL
PEERING	SAUNTERED	INVECTIVES	DENUNCIATION	CONTEMPTUOUS
WANED	NUANCE	FREE SPACE	DISSEMBLE	PATRONIZING
ENTHRALLED	IMPETUS	RITUAL	QUALMS	REVEL
CONTEMPLATE	RELENTLESSLY	INDULGENTLY	YEARNED	EMULATE

Black Boy Vocabulary

PETTY	DENUNCIATION	ARDENTLY	SURREPTITIOUSLY	INCONCEIVABLE
QUALMS	DELUSION	INTRIGUE	BOON	ASPIRATIONS
IMPUDENT	AVAILED	FREE SPACE	INDUCED	PRESUME
INCURRED	INVECTIVES	CONTEMPLATE	FRENZY	ANXIETY
DOUR	EMULATE	PREDILECTION	PLIABLE	SUBSERVIENCE

Black Boy Vocabulary

INDULGENTLY	HYPOTHETICAL	REPUGNANT	VINDICTIVE	LIEU
ANTAGONISM	DUBIOUS	NONCHALANTLY	SQUALOR	PATRONIZING
SAUNTERED	RELENTLESSLY	FREE SPACE	ACUTE	FIAT
SOLIDARITY	DEBASED	CRYPTIC	CONTEMPTUOUS	EXPLOITED
RITUAL	OBSTINACY	PROVOCATIONS	INTUITIVELY	SOLICITUDE

Black Boy Vocabulary

TANTAMOUNT	DENUNCIATION	SAUCILY	DELUSION	IMPLACABLE
FEIGNED	OBSTINACY	VIVID	DUBIOUS	INCONCEIVABLE
PETTY	DEVASTATED	FREE SPACE	PEERING	IMPETUS
BOON	ANTAGONISM	INDUCED	LIEU	OVERTONE
LARCENOUS	DISSEMBLE	FIAT	CONTEMPLATE	ENTHRALLED

Black Boy Vocabulary

DEBASED	ANXIETY	TAUT	ROUSED	REVEL
FRENZY	CONTEMPTUOUS	SOLIDARITY	CONSPICUOUSLY	PRESUME
DOUR	HYPOTHETICAL	FREE SPACE	RITUAL	MOROSE
BLASPHEMY	AVAILED	SURREPTITIOUSLY	IMPLORING	ARDENTLY
CRYPTIC	LIVID	NUANCE	BAFFLED	EXPLOITED

Black Boy Vocabulary

EXPLOITED	DISSEMBLE	SQUALOR	ARDENTLY	ACUTE
EMULATE	INTUITIVELY	RITUAL	WAYLAYING	TANTAMOUNT
VIVID	HYPOTHETICAL	FREE SPACE	DEVASTATED	OBSTINACY
FIAT	ROUSED	AVAILED	INCONCEIVABLE	MOROSE
PEERING	ANTAGONISM	INVECTIVES	DELUSION	AURA

Black Boy Vocabulary

LIEU	VINDICTIVE	ASPIRATIONS	BLASPHEMY	NONCHALANTLY
IMPUDENT	OVERTONE	ANXIETY	SURREPTITIOUSLY	REVEL
INTRIGUE	PATRONIZING	FREE SPACE	CRYPTIC	CONSPICUOUSLY
PLIABLE	DENUNCIATION	RECONDITE	CONTEMPLATE	CONTEMPTUOUS
SOLICITUDE	PREDILECTION	LIVID	DOUR	FEIGNED

Black Boy Vocabulary

RELENTLESSLY	LOITERING	WANED	VIVID	YEARNED
IMPETUS	DOUR	CRYPTIC	ASPIRATIONS	DISSEMBLE
TANTAMOUNT	NONCHALANTLY	FREE SPACE	DUBIOUS	ANXIETY
IMPLACABLE	PETTY	QUALMS	DEVOID	BLASPHEMY
VINDICTIVE	SUBSERVIENCE	INTUITIVELY	PEERING	AVAILED

Black Boy Vocabulary

PROVOCATIONS	INCURRED	DELUSION	REVEL	IMPUDENT
CONTEMPTUOUS	RECONDITE	ACUTE	INVECTIVES	LIEU
CONTEMPLATE	SOLICITUDE	FREE SPACE	FIAT	INCONCEIVABLE
MOROSE	CONSPICUOUSLY	ENTHRALLED	SOLIDARITY	EMULATE
AURA	PRESUME	SAUNTERED	HYPOTHETICAL	INDULGENTLY

Black Boy Vocabulary

ROUSED	PLIABLE	SOLIDARITY	CONTEMPTUOUS	ASPIRATIONS
REVEL	EMULATE	SURREPTITIOUSLY	DUBIOUS	YEARNED
IMPETUS	RECONDITE	FREE SPACE	QUALMS	IMPLACABLE
BOON	PEERING	BLASPHEMY	INCRIMINATING	NUANCE
SAUCILY	PREDILECTION	DELUSION	AVAILED	INCURRED

Black Boy Vocabulary

CONSPICUOUSLY	ACUTE	ANTAGONISM	VINDICTIVE	FEIGNED
DEBASED	DISSEMBLE	WANED	ENTHRALLED	SAUNTERED
TAUT	TANTAMOUNT	FREE SPACE	PROVOCATIONS	REPUGNANT
DEVASTATED	SQUALOR	LIEU	INVECTIVES	LOITERING
INCONCEIVABLE	RITUAL	FIAT	INTUITIVELY	BAFFLED

Black Boy Vocabulary

OBSTINACY	RELENTLESSLY	ENTHRALLED	ANXIETY	NONCHALANTLY
SURREPTITIOUSLY	WAYLAYING	INDULGENTLY	DEVOID	IMPUDENT
RECONDITE	BLASPHEMY	FREE SPACE	IMPLACABLE	NOSTALGIA
PROVOCATIONS	INVECTIVES	LARCENOUS	INCRIMINATING	DUBIOUS
RITUAL	DISSEMBLE	MOROSE	PLIABLE	IMPLORING

Black Boy Vocabulary

LIEU	REPUGNANT	CONTEMPLATE	INTRIGUE	BOON
EXPLOITED	FEIGNED	SAUNTERED	OVERTONE	TAUT
ANTAGONISM	CAPITULATE	FREE SPACE	DOUR	DELUSION
TANTAMOUNT	ASPIRATIONS	NUANCE	HYPOTHETICAL	QUALMS
YEARNED	PRESUME	FIAT	VIVID	SAUCILY

Black Boy Vocabulary

ASPIRATIONS	HYPOTHETICAL	ROUSED	IMPUDENT	PLIABLE
CONSPICUOUSLY	INVECTIVES	DISSEMBLE	FEIGNED	INCONCEIVABLE
PATRONIZING	ANXIETY	FREE SPACE	DENUNCIATION	EXPLOITED
QUALMS	DEVASTATED	ACUTE	DOUR	OVERTONE
CRYPTIC	LOITERING	TAUT	NOSTALGIA	SAUCILY

Black Boy Vocabulary

DUBIOUS	FRENZY	INCRIMINATING	PREDILECTION	INTRIGUE
IMPLORING	IMPETUS	PRESUME	BANTERING	LARCENOUS
INDULGENTLY	NONCHALANTLY	FREE SPACE	INTUITIVELY	REPUGNANT
DELUSION	LIVID	VINDICTIVE	IMPLACABLE	PETTY
TANTAMOUNT	RELENTLESSLY	SQUALOR	EMULATE	DEBASED

Black Boy Vocabulary

PRESUME	ANXIETY	FIAT	DEBASED	OBSTINACY
LIVID	CRYPTIC	CAPITULATE	BANTERING	TAUT
VINDICTIVE	AURA	FREE SPACE	VIVID	ARDENTLY
IMPLORING	RITUAL	BLASPHEMY	QUALMS	INVECTIVES
DENUNCIATION	ROUSED	BAFFLED	INCRIMINATING	HYPOTHETICAL

Black Boy Vocabulary

EMULATE	FRENZY	INTRIGUE	PLIABLE	ASPIRATIONS
IMPLACABLE	WANED	PETTY	REPUGNANT	TANTAMOUNT
SAUCILY	SAUNTERED	FREE SPACE	CONSPICUOUSLY	NONCHALANTLY
DUBIOUS	MOROSE	DOUR	EXPLOITED	INCONCEIVABLE
DISSEMBLE	SOLICITUDE	CONTEMPTUOUS	DEVASTATED	IMPETUS

Black Boy Vocabulary

NONCHALANTLY	CRYPTIC	BANTERING	FEIGNED	LIVID
PLIABLE	CONTEMPTUOUS	PATRONIZING	REPUGNANT	DEBASED
DENUNCIATION	BAFFLED	FREE SPACE	NUANCE	PREDILECTION
RITUAL	CAPITULATE	INTUITIVELY	RECONDITE	ENTHRALLED
IMPUDENT	ACUTE	AURA	NOSTALGIA	OBSTINACY

Black Boy Vocabulary

DELUSION	DEVASTATED	SURREPTITIOUSLY	INVECTIVES	ARDENTLY
IMPETUS	DUBIOUS	SOLICITUDE	MOROSE	QUALMS
VINDICTIVE	OVERTONE	FREE SPACE	CONTEMPLATE	PEERING
WAYLAYING	DOUR	LIEU	PRESUME	RELENTLESSLY
BOON	INCRIMINATING	REVEL	SUBSERVIENCE	HYPOTHETICAL

Black Boy Vocabulary

SOLICITUDE	YEARNED	VINDICTIVE	MOROSE	SAUCILY
FEIGNED	PETTY	TAUT	CONSPICUOUSLY	DOUR
SAUNTERED	RELENTLESSLY	FREE SPACE	WANED	INVECTIVES
IMPETUS	INCRIMINATING	LIVID	ANXIETY	REVEL
ARDENTLY	INCONCEIVABLE	INCURRED	OBSTINACY	PRESUME

Black Boy Vocabulary

NOSTALGIA	PLIABLE	EMULATE	CRYPTIC	DEVOID
AVAILED	DEBASED	PREDILECTION	BLASPHEMY	DELUSION
BAFFLED	VIVID	FREE SPACE	DENUNCIATION	QUALMS
LOITERING	ANTAGONISM	REPUGNANT	FRENZY	DISSEMBLE
PATRONIZING	LIEU	SUBSERVIENCE	NONCHALANTLY	ASPIRATIONS

Black Boy Vocabulary

SURREPTITIOUSLY	EMULATE	LIVID	YEARNED	AVAILED
INDUCED	DEBASED	ANTAGONISM	NUANCE	ROUSED
INCURRED	BOON	FREE SPACE	INDULGENTLY	VIVID
FEIGNED	INVECTIVES	CONTEMPTUOUS	ARDENTLY	EXPLOITED
DOUR	DEVOID	DELUSION	PREDILECTION	LOITERING

Black Boy Vocabulary

BLASPHEMY	REVEL	SOLICITUDE	PEERING	CAPITULATE
ASPIRATIONS	MOROSE	CONTEMPLATE	SAUCILY	PRESUME
RELENTLESSLY	PATRONIZING	FREE SPACE	FIAT	HYPOTHETICAL
OBSTINACY	OVERTONE	ACUTE	REPUGNANT	ANXIETY
BAFFLED	DEVASTATED	PLIABLE	DUBIOUS	SOLIDARITY

Black Boy Vocabulary

INTUITIVELY	EMULATE	CAPITULATE	PETTY	PROVOCATIONS
OVERTONE	BAFFLED	VINDICTIVE	TAUT	FRENZY
SAUNTERED	BANTERING	FREE SPACE	WAYLAYING	DUBIOUS
INDUCED	RELENTLESSLY	QUALMS	IMPLORING	ENTHRALLED
ACUTE	WANED	SQUALOR	PRESUME	RITUAL

Black Boy Vocabulary

HYPOTHETICAL	EXPLOITED	IMPLACABLE	DENUNCIATION	CONTEMPLATE
IMPETUS	PLIABLE	SAUCILY	INCRIMINATING	REPUGNANT
SURREPTITIOUSLY	PEERING	FREE SPACE	SOLICITUDE	CONTEMPTUOUS
DOUR	RECONDITE	ANTAGONISM	LOITERING	INCURRED
SOLIDARITY	NUANCE	ROUSED	REVEL	INVECTIVES

Black Boy Vocabulary

FEIGNED	BLASPHEMY	RECONDITE	PATRONIZING	CAPITULATE
INCURRED	NONCHALANTLY	WANED	AVAILED	ACUTE
VIVID	SAUCILY	FREE SPACE	FRENZY	EMULATE
DELUSION	MOROSE	DEVASTATED	PREDILECTION	CONSPICUOUSLY
QUALMS	OBSTINACY	ROUSED	NOSTALGIA	INDULGENTLY

Black Boy Vocabulary

IMPLORING	INCRIMINATING	SUBSERVIENCE	ANTAGONISM	BANTERING
DENUNCIATION	RITUAL	ARDENTLY	TANTAMOUNT	BOON
CONTEMPTUOUS	ANXIETY	FREE SPACE	LIVID	PEERING
PROVOCATIONS	IMPETUS	AURA	DISSEMBLE	FIAT
DEBASED	IMPUDENT	DUBIOUS	ENTHRALLED	PLIABLE

Black Boy Vocabulary

WAYLAYING	DENUNCIATION	SOLIDARITY	PEERING	YEARNED
MOROSE	OBSTINACY	IMPUDENT	INCONCEIVABLE	DELUSION
CRYPTIC	CONTEMPLATE	FREE SPACE	SUBSERVIENCE	BLASPHEMY
IMPETUS	PROVOCATIONS	LOITERING	QUALMS	ARDENTLY
ASPIRATIONS	AVAILED	NOSTALGIA	BOON	CAPITULATE

Black Boy Vocabulary

ENTHRALLED	DISSEMBLE	INDULGENTLY	INCRIMINATING	SOLICITUDE
AURA	DEVASTATED	PLIABLE	LIVID	LARCENOUS
DUBIOUS	FIAT	FREE SPACE	REVEL	ACUTE
TAUT	REPUGNANT	EMULATE	FEIGNED	INTRIGUE
DEVOID	SQUALOR	PATRONIZING	CONSPICUOUSLY	DOUR

www.ingramcontent.com/pod-product-compliance
Lightning Source LLC
Chambersburg PA
CBHW081452070526
44586CB00019B/2320